One Weekend
A Month - My Ass!

One Weekend
A Month - My Ass!

Edition II

Sgt. Joseph Berlin (ret.)

Library of Congress Control Number:		2009905240
ISBN:	Hardcover	978-1-4415-4084-3
	Softcover	978-1-4415-4083-6

To order additional copies of this book, contact:
Xlibris Corporation
1-888-795-4274
www.Xlibris.com
Orders@Xlibris.com
60261

This book is dedicated to my two daughters, Jennie and Christie, who suffered as well during this time in the year 2003.

This book is written from a collection of journal entries I kept during my training in the States before I went overseas to Iraq, and copies of letters I sent home to my daughters and school that I taught at when activated, as well as some stories that I wrote about my experiences. There are some facts that are wrong in this book but I kept them in because they were the truth to me at the time. The letters are mostly word for word as they were written and sent. I have included stories with details of events and places that I endured during the summer of 2003. There are pictures that go along with my writings that help to show, as well as explain, what I experienced. I have changed or omitted the names of people to protect their privacy. I was not a hero, nor was I involved in any large fighting that took place in Iraq. I was just a fifty-three year old man, close to my twenty-year letter for retirement in the National Guard, who happened to be sent to war in Iraq. I don't pretend to be brave or have any deep meaning to my experiences. I just want to share an average story of an average soldier in Iraq.

Sgt. Joseph Berlin (ret.)

Thursday / 1-9-2003

I have been activated for a week end of railhead training. I guess with the war getting close to starting in Iraq they need people who can load trucks, tanks, and equipment on the trains. I was activated in 1990 for the Gulf War and remember watching our trucks loaded on the train in Ft. Knox, Kentucky. They were all painted in the desert camouflage, tied down, and ready to roll. So, I guess this time and this war I'll be one of the people loading the equipment.

I drove to Camp Roberts, which is about halfway between San Francisco and Los Angeles. The base looks deserted. There is hardly anyone here. Of course, no one who was there knew where we were suppose to be. It's the typical Army stuff. There is never enough information and at the beginning of every event, and there never seems to be anyone who is in charge who knows their ass from a hole in the ground.

Eventually, we find our barracks around 1600. These barracks are the World War II variety. They are old, dirty, and run down. Paint is peeling, dirt is piled up in the corners, and the mattresses and pillows are all stained. I go upstairs and grab a bunk. I try to get a bunk that is away from the stairs so that I don't hear the drunks coming in all night and stomping up the stairway. Years of spending time in barracks have taught me that. I also went upstairs so I don't have to listen to the footsteps of people with no sense of time or noise during late night hours. The bathrooms, which are just a room with a row of sinks and a row of toilet bowls with a shower room, are always near the stairs, so by avoiding the stairway, you avoid the stink and noise of the bathroom.

After sitting around for an hour or so someone tells us which mess hall to go to in order to eat dinner. Of course, since the base is almost closed and there are only a few of us around, the meal is horrible! But, that is typical Army, too. Only on holidays or special occasions do the cooks put forth any effort at all to make a decent meal for the troops. So, after dinner I head for a club that is on the post. I drink a couple beers just to do something then head back to the barracks.

Back in the barracks I read a little and then listen to some music with my headphones. Everyone has their own way of spending their down-time. Some talk, some sleep, some read, some write, some listen to music, and some just sit there like zombies and do nothing. I finally fall asleep around 2230.

During the first night there I had to get up and piss three times. That's what I get for drinking a couple beers. While walking down the row of bunks in the barracks, down the stairs, and to the head, there are some guys watching movies on their computers that I pass. They are really loud and the beer cans around their bunks explains why. Getting a bunk on the top floor and away from the stairs is a handicap when you have to get up in the night because you drank some beer that evening.

The rumors so far is that no one knows what to expect and we might be here for two weeks. And so it begins.

Friday / 1-10-2003

Yikes! Woken up at 0500. I'm in the Army again. We ate a lousy breakfast, as usual, and head to class at 0800. Of course, the class didn't start until 0900, but it was nice to just stand around and try to wake up a little more before sitting in a room listening to someone talk for hours about something they probably haven't done before and only read about it in a manual.

The class goes all right but I am tired. It's hard to get decent rest when you have to leave your own bed at home and try to sleep in an old barracks with about fifty other guys. And let's not forget about laying on a mattress that is so stained that you wonder if they bought it from a whore house. The thickness of the mattress is about an inch and the springs under it are nothing more than a bunch of curled wires tied together. You're lucky if all the hooks that keep the springs tied to the frame are there. There is always some major sagging going on when you lay down on those bunks.

We got an hour and a half for lunch, which is really good. Usually, it's no longer than an hour so anything extra makes you feel like you're getting away with something. Getting away with something in the Army is something that everyone does, especially in the Guard.

We were done at 1600 and I didn't even bother going to the mess hall for chow. I went straight to the club and had some pizza and beer. The club would become a regular thing for me as I just couldn't stand eating that slop in the mess hall day after day.

Back in the barracks it was the same as always. I read some, listened to some music, and fell asleep after 0100. The guys are drinking more tonight and louder than last night. National Guard mentality is starting to show.

Sunday / 1-11-2003

Class is over and I'm sent home. I don't know shit about loading any railcars. All I did was sleep in a shitty bed for two nights in a shitty old barracks and eat bad food. The fucking Guard comes through again. I'm suppose to wait to hear something about activation soon but go home. What a fucking waste of my time!

ACTIVATION FOR IRAQ

Friday / 2-7-2003

I had to be at my National Guard Armory in Van Nuys at 0700. That means getting up around 0400 at home, getting the uniform on, and driving down from Ventura, California. It's about a one hour drive but you never know how the traffic will be on the freeways of California.

A group of us are going to convoy from the Van Nuys Armory to Camp Roberts. We'll take three Hummers with our gear. I'm the NCOIC (Non Commissioned Officer in Charge). The title doesn't mean shit unless something goes wrong, then I get blamed. So, we TM (technical maintenance) the trucks and head out.

On the way to Camp Roberts I take the small convoy off the freeway and stop at my house in Ventura. I wanted to show off for my two daughters and also the neighborhood. This man was going to war in Iraq and I wanted three Army Hummers to stop in front of my house and make everyone take notice. I was feeling very macho right about then. Of course, my daughters weren't home and hardly any neighbors saw me and the trucks, at least as far as I could tell. So, with a little smaller dick than when I started, we loaded back up and took off.

It took about six hours to get to Camp Roberts. We found our barracks, still the old World War II type, which was all that was at Camp Roberts. Everyone bunked down and I went to sleep around 2200.

Saturday / 2-8-2003

I'm up at 0500 and off to chow. The one meal that the cooks in the Army can't mess up too much is breakfast, so I'm grateful for that.

We went to a class about something that I can't remember. It's always the same. Some guy gets tasked with giving a class. So, the guy gets a manual and starts reading from it. It's the most boring way in the world to learn anything and that's why we don't learn anything from these stupid fucking classes.

It is cold as hell here in the mornings. Everyone is laughing that we'll be going to a desert environment and we're training in the winter in California with the temperature going down in the thirty-degree range. Crazy! It does warm up around 1000.

The rumor for today is that we are not going to Iraq. Rumors are like farts in the Army. There is always one hanging around and you know another one is on the way soon. Most rumors stink just as the Army farts stink. Yesterday's rumor was we are getting the orders to go seventy-two hours after we get home from this training. I'm feeling that we will go, but who knows what at this point is unknown. No use worrying about something I have no control over anyway.

We marched to our trucks out in the parking lot and sat around until lunch. I'm not sure what that was suppose to accomplish but it was prime bullshitting time. MREs (meals ready to eat) for lunch. The only MRE that I can stomach is one with barbecue sauce. All the others are awful. I try and get to the case of MREs and search through them but there is usually someone standing there yelling at you to just take one and get the fuck out of the way. Stupid Army! Don't they know I must have my barbecue?

The classes in the afternoon are the same as in the morning. Stupid with stupid instructors. Of course, I don't tell anyone in charge that I'm a teacher in civilian life or they'll make me teach all the classes even though I don't know shit about the subjects. Better to stand to the side and be silent than to be in front of the group and prove that you're useless.

Today was a complete bullshit Army day. Nothing got done, nothing was learned. All I know is that I have to be here and endure.

Sunday / 2-9-2003

Today started out without any inclination that it would turn out to be totally fucked up. The Army has a saying which is, "SNAFU." It means, "situation normal, all fucked up."

We were introduced to our M1070 Heavy Equipment Transporter or HET. These are the trucks that our company will be driving over in Iraq. They are the largest trucks in the Army. The official explanation of these trucks is that the HETS transports payloads up to seventy tons—primarily Abrams tanks. The tractor and trailer weigh twenty-seven tons. It's job is to transport, deploy, recover and evacuate combat-loaded main battle tanks and other heavy tracked and wheeled vehicles to and from the battlefield. Impressive, huh?

We are suppose to drive the trucks around a little to get used to them. Can you imagine getting behind the wheel of a truck that is about two stories high, with a trailer that has forty wheels, that you've never seen before and driving it? That's how the Army does things. Don't worry about learning about the truck, just get behind the wheel and drive the damn thing. No problem.

We drive around the parade ground in circles and just raise a lot of dust. The truck is really easy to drive despite the fact it is so large. The Army has made sure that the dumbest fuck could drive any truck they have. It's automatic so you just put it in gear and steer.

After half the day we are told to go to our barracks, change into our PT (physical training) clothes, and wait.

We are marched to a gym at 1500. There are three companies here getting prepared to go to Iraq. All three companies are marching on the road up to the gym. There is someone calling cadence so we can be in step as we march, but most of us can't hear the person and we are all out of step. I hope no one is watching because we look like a mob walking down the road instead of troops marching to a destination. Some of the guys are laughing and talking, not taking anything serious at all. The National Guard at it's finest. We march into the gym and are told where to stand. They pack us in like sardines. There are three hundred troops in my company alone so when the other two companies are crammed in, there is very little room to move. We are told to sit down. So, here are about eleven hundred troops in their shorts and t-shirts sitting on a gym floor wondering what the hell is going on.

A general walks in and someone yells, "Attention!" We all scramble to our feet knocking into each other and trying to stand still. The general walks to the front of the gym and tells us to "Take a seat!"

That's when the Iraq program begins. The general tells us that the war is coming and we are going to be in it. He tells us what a great adventure it will be and an honor to be serving our country when called upon. It sounds great and we are geared up to believe every word. He goes on and on about duty, honor, and country and we soak it up.

An officer walks in with his face painted in camouflage. He starts yelling about fighting in a war and how we will have to learn how to fight. He is an embarrassment! He looks stupid walking around yelling. We're in a fucking gym sitting in shorts and this guy is yelling at us about being tough. Shit! I hate the Army when it's this bullshit.

They have a band playing marching songs in the corner as we marched in and as we marched out. I guess this program is suppose to fire us up about going to war. It's funny, but it works.

The general tells us that our orders are in and we are to be activated on February 14th. Happy Valentine's Day. We will train at Camp Roberts, then at Ft. Lewis, Washington, then we'll be sent to the Middle East. That was fast! We are told that our transportation company will be sent overseas first. Figures.

We march outside, line up, and march back to our barracks. Everyone is talking like crazy and hoping that they will send us home so we can spend some time with our families before being activated for the war. What the fuck am I getting into?

Monday / 2-10-2003

They had a medical screening at 2200 today. My blood pressure is too high to be considered for activation. Shit! I don't know how the fuck they expect my blood pressure to be normal. They dick with me all day. They feed me shit. I'm surrounded by idiots. I don't get any sleep because I'm in a barracks with fifty guys snoring, talking, and being stupid-ass drunks all night. They tell me I'm going to war and they tell me to relax and stay calm? What a bunch of assholes. So, I have to be tested again at 0700 tomorrow. Sometimes I hate the Army.

I don't know if I'll be going or not. I'm sure my two daughters will be happy as well as my Mom, but this is embarrassing.

Tuesday / 2-11-2003

I went to get my blood pressure retaken at 0700. I passed this time. I guess it was too early in the day for me to get all bent out of shape and pissed off. Not enough time in the day to have stupid-ass things happen. To take the test still took two hours so I'm surprised I didn't hit the high scores again after standing around for that length of time.

We convoyed home and I arrived back home about 1400. Now I get two days to spend with my girls before I have to take off for a long time. Rumor is that we'll be gone for over one year. I can't believe this is happening to me. I'm fifty-three fucking years old, out of shape, and in the last year before I can retire with twenty years in the service and they are sending me to war in Iraq. Holly fucking shit!

Wednesday / 2-12-2003

I took the girls to Santa Barbara to spend one last evening together. Of course we ended up in a bar. My daughters were proud of me and told everyone that I was going off to Iraq to fight the good fight. We got a lot of free drinks that night. Of course, my two daughters got hammered. By the end of the night, one was passed out on a bench in the bar and the other one was singing on stage with a stranger. I had to herd them up and out and back to the motel room. It was like herding cats. Once I had one moving the other one would disappear. It was a miracle we made it back at all that night. Great memories for a future warrior.

Thursday / 2-13-2003

I spent the day packing my gear and last minute details. The girls are too wiped out to show any emotion today. It's a good thing because it was hard enough getting ready to leave them for over a year and a war halfway around the world. I still can't believe this is happening.

Friday / 2-14-2003

This is one of the toughest days of my life. I got up at 0430. My daughters and I drove to Van Nuys where I load on a bus for a ride to Lancaster (the town where our company was meeting for the ride to Camp Roberts). My girls follow the bus in my car.

We arrive at 0800 and the girls are hugging me. We just sit and hug and make small talk. We are all just trying to hold it together for the moment.

We are finally told to get on the bus. My name is called and I break free from my daughters' hold. I tell them I love them and climb on the bus. As I take a seat by the window I look outside and see my oldest daughter standing at the rear of my car crying like a baby. My youngest is standing closer to the bus and crying as a female soldier holds her. Both daughter's faces are red and wet. I begin to cry. I try not to and I try to be tough, but I can't hold it in. Tears are running down my face, my girls are crying, as well as most of the people standing there around the bus. It's a miserable feeling and a hopeless one, too.

The bus is finally loaded and we start to drive away. People are waving and crying as well as most of the soldiers on the bus. Kids are yelling for their daddies and mommies and waving. My two daughters are a mess. I hide my face and my tears and look away.

I don't remember much of the bus ride to Camp Roberts. Everything is a blur this day. Everyone is hurting inside but trying to be tough so the talking is louder than usual and the laughs seemed more forced. I feel like shit!

Happy fucking Valentine's Day!

Saturday / 2-15-2003

We get up at 0500. We have classes called CTT for 'Common Task Training.' It's skills that are basic for every soldier to learn, your rifle, first aid, gear, etc. Same old Army. Some guy is in front of about fifty soldiers who don't give a shit about whatever the subject is, reading right from the manual like a fucking robot. No one is listening. We are all glad that we are just sitting around in the barracks doing nothing. I even get picked to give a class on first aid because someone found out that I was a medic back in my active Army days from 1969-71. Like I can remember anything from thirty years ago. So, I read from the manual as no one listens to me. I can't blame them. I do the same thing when someone else is teaching a class.

After a full day of bullshit classes in the barracks and MREs for lunch we head out to the field (this is what we call going out into the woods or any training site in the Army) to practice a tactical move. We get in our pick ups and Humvees and pretend we are driving into a hostile AO (area of operations).

We park our trucks and Hummers and lay in the grass pretending we are protecting ourselves from the enemy. We don't even have our weapons. We lay there like lumps of shit just because someone wants us to play at war instead of letting us go for the night. So, I lay in the wet grass and close my eyes and try to sleep. It's a fucking joke and I'm in the middle of it.

We get back to the barracks at 1930 and do our thing. What tomorrow brings, I don't know.

Sunday 2-16-2003

Today we spent in the field. The convoy left the camp at 1000. We actually took our weapons with us. It's been a while since I had to carry around an M-16 all day. In the morning we just sat around in the grass and bitched about everything. On our tactical convoy move we were ambushed by our evaluators with gas. It was a total cluster fuck! We stopped our trucks and got out. You have eight seconds to get your mask on and it took me about fifty. Once you get your mask on you're suppose to lay down and point your weapon out toward the enemy. So, there is a cloud of gas somewhere off to our side, we are all laying in the grass trying to get the rocks out from under our crotches, and holding our weapons pointed out. No one does anything even though we can hear shooting in the distance. I can't see shit. It's just a nice sunny day in California and I'm laying in the grass pretending to be at war.

During our after-action report (where the leaders tell us how shitty we did and how fucked up we are) we got reamed. I don't think we did one thing right. It's funny because if you're in a truck and someone throws gas at you why the hell would you stop? Unless they blow a truck up, you just keep going to get out of the kill-zone. But, we stopped. Stupid! That just lets the bad guys shoot at you while you're not moving.

We had to spend the night in our trucks out in the field. It was cold and I was laying in the back bench of the cab with my field jacket on trying to stay warm. Of course, our wonderful evaluators attacked us about 0200. A lot of guys went out and pretended to fight but I just stayed in the back of my cab laying down. Being in the National Guard and in a camp in California, I knew no one would miss me and why the hell should I go running around in the dark when I was nice and comfortable where I was? It worked out perfectly because when the other guys came back they didn't see anything and didn't have a clue as to what the hell was going on. I didn't miss a thing.

They woke us up at 0400 and we drove back to the base. Our ramp on our trailer broke and we dragged it through the mud for miles. When you're driving a truck as big as the one we were, you can't even tell if something is broke on the truck. I had no idea until we arrived at camp and the driver behind us explained how we had dragged our ramp behind us.

We leave for Ft. Lewis, Washington on the 20th.

Wednesday / 2-19-2003

It's been an interesting few days since I last wrote an entry in my journal. We had a lot of classes on CT. We got to go through a gas chamber with the TV news present. This going to war in Iraq is still rather new to Americans right now. The gas chamber is nothing but a tent set up in the field. After putting your mask on outside you walk inside the tent in a group and stand around a little table set up in the middle. Some guy already in his mask is waiting for us. This is one time you really try make sure your mask is on right because you know if you don't, you will pay. He starts the gas and you just stand there. You wait and wait and hope your eyes don't start watering up or you start coughing. If you do, that means your mask leaks. After a while they ask if anyone wants to take their mask off inside the tent. A few idiots do. I don't know what the hell they are trying to prove, but I don't volunteer. We watch the assholes start to cough and gag and then we all walk out of the tent. Outside the TV cameras are all over us. Of course they focus in on the assholes who took their masks off in the tent and are now red in the face, coughing, with their eyes watering, and snot coming out of their noses. Funny, but the TV people like idiots. Makes for better television.

There is a guy in our platoon who drives a truck in civilian life. He's a typical redneck. We are finding out that he is a total drunk, too. He has the bunk right next to mine on the upper floor. He came in so drunk on one of these past nights that he just laid in his bed and passed out. About an hour after he collapsed he started puking. But, he pukes a little different than anyone I had ever seen before. He pukes into his bunk where his face is and doesn't get out of it. He just pukes and pukes and pukes and lays there. The place is reeking of puke and some of the guys jump up to help him. I help him because I don't want to be thought of as someone who doesn't give a shit (but really, I don't give a shit). After they get him up and down to the bathroom to clean him up, I'm sitting there looking at his bunk with puke all over it. I'm gagging myself now. So, I get my gear and head downstairs to look for a free bunk to move to. It was one of the better moves I ever made in this activation. Little did I know that this same guy would do the same thing later on in his cot on the back of his truck in Iraq.

One of the nights I went to the laundry mat they have here on base to wash my clothes. A couple friends and I took some beer with us and drank them pretty fast. We talked about the women we had in our lives and laughed about a lot of dirty stories. It was a pretty good time.

Tonight we are all packing our bags for the trip to Ft. Lewis tomorrow. I could barely fit everything into the two duffle bags I had. One bag is for a trailer and the other bag is for the bus. Both bags will end up on the plane so I don't know what the fuck the difference is, but I go along.

Rumors are flying around like crazy. They have us going from Panama, to Florida, to staying in Ft. Lewis, to Kuwait. No one really knows what the hell is going to happen, but some of these people sure like to sound like they do. We'll see.

Thursday / 2-20-2003

We sat around all day until it was time to load up on the buses for our trip to the airport. We loaded up at 1800 and headed for Monterey. Once we got there we had to sit and wait on the buses. The ride there was crowded and cramped and just sitting there didn't help. There were two different flights and of course, I was on the second one. So, I got to sit on the bus even longer and watch my feet swell up. After waiting on the tarmac until 2400 we finally took off for Ft. Lewis, Washington.

We arrived at Ft. Lewis at 0300 and moved into some more buses for the ride to the barracks. Once we arrived at our barracks we had to wait for the trucks to show up with the bags so we can unload them and get our gear. Again the gods are looking down on me and pissing on me as my bag is on the second truck to arrive. I don't get to sleep until 0500. The only good thing is that these barracks, although still the old World War II style, have better bunks and mattresses and I am happy as I fall asleep.

Friday / 2-21-2003

What the hell? They let us sleep until 0900. Are they getting weak? That is a lot later than I was expecting. A whole four hours sleep.

We have a formation and then they tell us to wait. We sit around in the barracks and shoot the shit and wait.

At 1030 we have another formation and are moving out to get our active Army ID cards.

After lunch we are taken to a building where we are to get more gear such as our flak vests, back packs, rain gear, cold weather boots (where the hell is this war again), etc. They are out of everything. The supplies they have are old and worn. I don't get a back pack but I get the frame. Fucking hilarious! My flak vest is dirty and the old Viet Nam style that can't even stop a bullet. If America could see how shitty the National Guard is being treated this country would be embarrassed. I guess it's OK for me to go to war with second hand equipment that won't be as good as the active Army's gear because we're just the National Guard. You know, "Week End Warriors." What a crock of shit!

We're back in the barracks by 1900 and good things happen. There is a pizza wagon that comes to our barracks. The guys are going crazy! Pizza right to the door of the barracks and it taste good. I think every person in the company bought their own pizza that night. And there are soda machines everywhere. We are in food heaven.

We spend the night putting what new gear we have together. There is gear everywhere mixed in with empty pizza boxes and soda cans. There was some major burping and farting going on this night.

Throughout the book I will include letters that match the dates of my journal entries. Here is the first letter.

Letter to the school I was teaching at when I was activated / 2-21-2003

Hey Everyone,
    Greetings from beautiful, rainy, cloudy, cold, boring Ft. Lewis, WA in Tacoma. I get up every day at 5 AM (sometimes earlier), even weekends, run around outside, drive our big trucks, train on skills, and get very little sleep. I have blisters on both

feet, a swollen knee, sores on my hands, and fall asleep within seconds of lying down. But, I wouldn't change it for anything. The troops are upbeat and preparing for whatever the future holds. I should be in Camp Doha in Kuwait in about three weeks. I hope my class is doing their best to make me and themselves proud. I will try to make them proud of me.

I miss the students and staff at school.

Mr. B.

P.S. Don't write to this address—by the time it gets here I'll probably be gone. More to follow . . .

Saturday / 2-22-2003

Today is SRP. I don't know what the hell that stands for (something about soldier readiness) but it's a bunch of stations that we all have to go through to get our paperwork and medical done prior to going to Iraq. We stand in a line for hours upon hours with a folder in our hands. On the folder is a list of places we have to visit and get initialed. Some of the stations are for wills, next of kin, what do with your body if you're killed. Others have to do with the medical side, as in blood pressure, blood type, eye check up, etc.

I cheat on the eye test. I have a lazy right eye and never do well with these eye tests. But, I catch a break. Just as I'm standing at the machine to look into for the test the examiner gets distracted by someone else. So, I hurriedly peak into the machine with my good left eye and write the letters down on my hand. When the test starts it works perfectly. Instead of reading the letters with my right eye, the bad one, I actually look down at my hand and read off of it. Passed with flying colors. So what if I'm blind in one eye and can't see shit with it?

Another station is one where they ask about your family information. I happen to be the last male with the name of Berlin in my family. There is a row of boxes that are to be checked "Go" or "No Go." When the soldier asks me if I would like to be deferred because I'm the last survivor with my name I realize that I have a way out. But, having no idea what is in store for me once I actually get to Iraq, I tell him "No." I often look back that that decision with some regret.

Then there is the station where you are sent for some shots. Smallpox is nothing but the Anthrax is really painful. Right in the back of the upper arm and it hurt like hell.

All I remember about this day is standing in line after line and trying like hell to get each station done. It seemed to never end.

Sunday / 2-23-2003

Today was basically a day to ourselves. Our fearless leaders did have one formation at 1600 just so they could fuck with us at least once this day. Otherwise, I went to the PX and walked around and had a good day. This base is really big compared to Camp Roberts back in California. There are a shit-load of soldiers everywhere, too.

I think the symptoms from the Anthrax are setting in. I was told we'd get "flu-like" symptoms and I feel like shit right now.

Monday / 2-24-2003

Common tasks training all morning. Boring, as usual. We sit around on our bunks and the floor while some guy reads from the manual. No one is listening. We're just trying to stay awake.

In the afternoon we are going through a series of what the Army calls, "briefs." It's where they tell you a bunch of stuff like the 'rules of engagement' and what to expect in Iraq. We also end up practicing marching. Shit! I haven't done any of that since I was in basic training about a zillion years ago (really, it was in 1969 when I was in basic training). Everyone is trying but we are not doing well. Even the guy yelling the marching orders is messing up big time. So, we go through the game of marching around like soldiers but we really just want to go lay down and sleep.

I feel lousy as hell. I'm really feeling sick. I don't know if it's from the anthrax shot or if I'm just getting ill. It's really cold here in Ft. Lewis. The temperature has been below freezing in the early morning.

Some of these guys are starting to get to me because they are so stupid. It's hard to watch someone be in charge who is probably some piss-ant in civilian life but in the Army has some rank and power. You can tell the idiots because they are always the dumbest, loudest, pricks around. Rank in the Army usually goes straight to the head and when there is not much in the head to begin with, that's an insane combination.

My young friend, who I call Barbara, told his "tea-bag" joke. Fucking hilarious! A hint . . . it's about dangling balls.

The talk is still about war. We'll see.

Tuesday / 2-25-2003

I'm really sick today. Ahhhh!

More bullshit CT classes. Map reading, claymore mines, weapons, foxholes, etc. Geez, what a fucking bore. Did they forget we're truckers?

I tried to answer some emails and the computer went down and I lost them all. Things aren't going very well lately.

We're going to the rifle range tomorrow. I have to pack my gear to be ready to spend the entire day outside with no cover. It's going to be cold and very long day.

Our instructors here are still teaching stupid shit that we don't need. I get frustrated with all the soldiers who are "instructors" who can't find their ass with both hands telling me how to do things. Stupid Army!

The latest rumor? We will go back to Camp Roberts in California and drive our own HETS to the port in Texas where they will be shipped to Kuwait. What a fucking joke. I can just imagine a bunch of guys who have only driven these monster trucks around in circles or in the mud roads of Camp Roberts driving down the highways of America. We will destroy everything we come into contact with and probably kill people on the way. What makes the Army think we are ready to drive these trucks that far when we have only driven them a few times?

Wednesday / 2-26-2003

What an Army day! We got up at 0400. It was fucking cold outside. We drew (signed out) our M-16s at 0500. Standing in line in the dark in the fucking cold was such a treat. Then they loaded us up on what is known as "cattle cars." These are trailers that are pulled by a truck. It's nothing but a big metal box that has some benches on the sides and a few rails to hold onto. There are seats for about twenty but we are crammed in with about forty of us. So, naturally, some are standing and leaning on the knees of those who were lucky enough to get seats. Here we are with our rifles, backpacks, a shit load of clothing including cold weather boots, banging around in a metal box that could easily hold cattle. Thus, the nickname, "Cattle cars." The ride to the range is miserable as we are all cold, uncomfortable, and banging into each other every time the truck hits a rut. Since we are headed into the field and it's been raining here for days, there are plenty of ruts for this driver to hit.

With my fifty-three year old eyes and the fact that I haven't fired my weapon in a long time, I had a lot of difficulty zeroing in. To zero means to set your sites up for your personal eyesight. You get three bullets to put as close together on the target as possible. When you get three in a particular small circle you have "zeroed." I was all over the place. I would get two close and third would disappear into the galaxy somewhere. Finally the instructor held a piece of cardboard over the eye I wasn't looking down the site with and I did it. Apparently I was keeping my other eye open while I sighted down the barrel and it was messing me up big-time. So, once I zeroed, I was put on a truck and taken down to the qualifying range.

By the time I got to the qualifying range it was almost dark. They have "pop-up" targets. These are black silhouettes that are raised up electronically and when your bullet hits it, it falls down. Then your score is recorded by a computer and you learn how you did after the forty rounds you get to fire. I can't even see half of the targets in the woods because it's twilight and the targets are black. This should be good. We fire at our targets and I swear I didn't even see most of them. We are told that we qualified and are off to another range for night firing. Now, I know I didn't hit shit that night, not only because it was dark out, but I'm a lousy shot. I'm pretty sure that we qualified because there was no more time in the day to have another cycle of firing and in order to go to war, you have to qualify with your M-16.

We are trucked to a small range where we will experience "night firing." We are issued ammunition with tracers. These are bullets that leave a red trail in the dark so you can see where you are shooting at night. It also lets the enemy know where you are because they can see the trajectory of the bullets, too. This is actually fun. They wait until it is completely dark. We walk up on line to the firing range. We lay down and are told to fire in front of us. At first there is controlled firing. Everyone is firing one bullet at a time and trying to aim as if something is in front of us. Then the instructor yells to "just shoot the fucking rounds down range as fast as you can." and we open up. Within seconds the red tracers are flying downrange and it looks like the 4th of July. Awesome!

We get back to the barracks at 2100 after marching for a few miles. It's been a long, cold, hard day and everyone is putting their gear away and trying to dry out some of it by laying in on the ends of the bunks and foot lockers we have. There is gear everywhere. We are wound up and dead tired at the same time. Once in a while you have a day like today in the Army. I'm beat!

Thursday / 2-27-2003

Today I joined an exclusive club. I joined the "Ma-Duce" club. The "Ma-Duce" club means I got picked to be part of the 50 caliber machine gun team. There is the gunner, which is my battle-buddy (a term the Army uses for the one person that you are suppose to be with and take care of at all times while deployed overseas), and the assistant gunner, or AG, which is me.

During the morning we went through classes to learn about the 50 cal. It's an awesome gun and it's very heavy. Just the tripod (legs) alone make me feel like a feeble old man. That's the part I will carry while my gunner will carry the machine gun itself. We learned how to clean the 50 cal as well as dismantle it and fire it. There is a "timing" thing that has to be just so for the machine gun to fire and I am having a little trouble understanding that part. Hell, just 'racking' (pulling back the bolt to inject a round or bullet) is hard for me. The young strong guys rack it easy and I'm yanking on it like I'm in a tug of war with fifty other people on the other side of the rope. This could be bad.

In the afternoon we were tested on our knowledge of the 50 cal and spent the rest of the time cleaning our M-16s from the previous days firing.

I went to the PX (post exchange) but didn't get anything. I just sort of stared at the women walking around and dreamed of being younger and cuter. I'm getting sick of all these guys and life in the barracks. I passed a gas station on base while I was on the bus ride back to the barracks and thought how cool it was. That's how much my life is changing, that I think a gas station is cool to see. What the Fuck?

Friday / 2-28-2003

I went to the range to qualify on the Ma-Duce. What a blast! Of course the range is wet and it's pretty cold, but walking with the 50 cal on our shoulders and heading for the firing points, I'm starting to feel like a real badass.

First, we have to zero in. We are given targets that are about 25 meters in front of us. The idea is to put a series of rounds into the target in a certain area. Once you can do that you know how to aim and shoot your 50 cal. It's a clusterfuck! I just shoot the shit out of the target and I don't even know how I hit it. The machine gun is loud and badass. Everyone pretty much does the same thing and after a while the instructor tells us we're ready for record firing.

We move out to the 50 cal range and set up our foxhole. This is a cement tube that is sunk into the ground with a platform in the middle for the Ma-Duce. I feel so good! I am muddy from crawling around in the wet sand, I have a cut on my hand, and I am about to shoot a really destructive gun, and I love it! I feel like a kid with a great new toy and I'll worry about going home all dirty to Ma later. Right now, I'm enjoying the shit out of this.

First my gunner gets to fire. I am suppose to watch the band of 50 cal bullets, which are fucking huge, to make sure they don't get tangled. I also am suppose to hold some elevation handle on the gun so the Ma-Duce doesn't swing wild in the gunners hands. After a few rounds, I am told to loosen the handle and the gunner gets to free-aim at his targets. There are a few targets down range that we can shoot at and the noise and impact of the rounds is just incredible.

Now it's my turn to shoot. I am so excited I can hardly keep from cumming in my pants. I shoot my first series of rounds down range while my battle-buddy holds the elevation handle. You're suppose to shoot off a series of three rounds and then let up on the trigger. It's not hard but the desire to just hold down the trigger and let 'em fly is tempting. I'm waiting for the instructor to tell my buddy to let go of the handle so I can fire on my own. He never does and I end up firing all my rounds while my assistant gunner half controls the gun. I'm really disappointed that I did not get to fire on my own. As the instructor comes back to my foxhole I ask him if I can fire some more rounds without my AG. He tells me I should have done that on my own and I don't have any more rounds to fire. Shit! I should have known that. I should have just done it on my own. I've been around the Army long enough to know better than to just think the instructors are in complete control of everything I do. Damn it!

I'm firing the 50 cal in Ft. Lewis

My battle-buddy and I work the Ma-Duce

We got back to the barracks at 2000 after stating the day out at 0500. I'm really tired, but in a weird way, happy.

I talked to my daughters on the phone. My youngest, Christie, had me in tears. She said, "Daddy, don't go." and I just lost it. My daughters are both adults in their twenties, but they are still my babies. This part is hard and it crashes me down to earth after my 50 cal high.

Saturday / 3-1-2003

Holy Shit! They are giving us a day off. I get to rest all day. Tonight a few of us are headed to Seattle for some fun.

After getting a room with all five of us staying in the same room we took a ride downtown Seattle. Of course we ended up in a strip club. I spent way too much money pretending that these hot, young women wanted me and thought I was the sexiest man alive. Isn't it amazing what a little booze and having a dick will do to us? We didn't get back to the room until 0400.

Back in the room I spend a long time in the shower for two reasons. One is because I haven't had any privacy in a few weeks and the other has to do with the fact I just left a strip club.

Sunday / 3-2-2003

Today we played the tourists. We visited the Space Needle, a Russian sub, the walkway along the water, and a bunch of shops. Then we headed back to hell. It rained all day today.

Monday / 3-3-2003

CTT all day today. There were classes on first aid, rifle maintenance, digging foxholes, and gas (no, not farts, riot gas) and masking skills. It was hard to stay awake after the week end of no sleep.

I had guard duty from 1600-2000. All I did was sit in a room with another guy and answer the phone and talk. Actually, I had enough time to write eight letters. So this guard duty was actually just a nice quiet place for me to relax for four hours.

Today's rumor is that we are headed back to Camp Roberts in California soon. I don't think anyone really knows where we'll be going, but I listen to the rumors and repeat them anyway.

I am really sick. I was up all last night coughing and it's getting worse. In fact, it seems like the entire company is getting sick. It's hard not to pass around the illness when you all live right on top of each other. There are about forty guys in my barracks on my floor alone. We sleep in double bunks and there isn't much room between them. What one gets the others get.

Laying in bed tonight I can't help thinking of a particular woman I know back home. She's kind of my young, hot, "I get to lay you once in a while" friend. She's the sexiest woman I've ever known, body-wise, but we're never going to have an actual relationship. But, right now, this night, I really miss her. I could use some fun with a woman right about now. These people and living in the barracks are starting to really get to me.

Letter to school written on guard duty / 3-3-2003

Hey Everyone,

Greeting from Ft. Lewis, Washington. It's still cold and rainy here. Why do people live in Seattle? I sure do miss our Southern California weather. I'll write what's been happening lately and you can share whatever you think is appropriate with my students and the staff.

I get up every day at 5 AM. Even Sundays are training days for us. We practice our skills to be able to do our jobs in the Army. Some skills are boring, but they are all important. We have weapons training, chemical and gas mask training, map reading, radio procedures, and other basic skills every soldier who may go to Iraq needs.

The last we heard is that we will be sent to Camp Doha, Kuwait in a few weeks, but rumors change every day here.

I miss my family, my apartment, my TV, and especially my bed. I miss all the great people at school, too!

Short note to B. (a teacher who was in contact with my girls while I was gone), could you please give a call to my girls for a little encouragement? A couple of times I've called and my oldest has been crying. Thanks. I won't forget.

Please write if you want. If I leave before the mail gets here, it will catch up.

Yours,
Joe Berlin (Mr. B.)

Thursday / 3-4-2003

We got up at 0400 today. I couldn't sleep last night because I'm coughing all the time now.

We went to the gas chamber today. It was a tent set up on a small hill. Walking up the road to the tent I passed the guys coming out of the tent. Most of them were all right but there were the idiots who took their masks off in the tent to play macho-man and the tears and snot were running down their faces. I hate going into the gas chamber.

We go in the tent and we walked in with the masks on this time. They have so much riot gas going in the tent that it looks like you are in the middle of a cloud. It doesn't take long to realize that my mask is leaking. My eyes start to water and I start coughing like crazy. I've been coughing because I'm sick, but this is different. I walk out of the tent and rip my mask off. My eyes are all fucked up and I'm sure I'm the one with snot running down his nose this time. An instructor comes over and helps me. We check my filters and refit the mask to my face. By putting your hands over the air intakes and taking a breath you can tell if your mask is secure because it collapses around your face. So, I go back into the tent and spend my few minutes. The mask works this time but when I come out, and for the next couple hours, my right eye and forehead is all fucked up.

We then went to classes about tactics. There are rules of engagement to learn, and setting up a perimeter, and the defense of it. There are other things we will have to train about and we are told we will spend the next three days at what is known as "lane training." So, I'll be playing at war for a few days to prepare for actually going to a war. It's getting too weird for me.

I took some medicine when I got back to the barracks and finally fell asleep about 2000. The medicine helped until about 2400 and then I was up coughing again. Damn it! I slept on and off all night again.

Wednesday / 3-5-2003

We're up at 0500. We have to wear our battle-rattle. This is all the combat gear we have. We put on out belts with the harness. On the belt we carry our canteen, two ammo pouches, and a first aid packet. We also have to wear our flak vest and Kevlar (helmet). I wear every piece of cold weather and rain weather gear I have. Over boots, rain pants and shirt, gloves, scarf, wool hat, and poncho are going with me. We're headed for the field for the entire day and the weather is cold and rainy.

After we draw, or sign out, our M-16s I'm told to get the Ma-Duce. You've got to be shitting me. What bullshit! My platoon sergeant is staring to be a real dick. No other platoon has to take the 50 cal out to the field today but ours. That means that my battle buddy and I will have to lug this monster around all day in the rain and mud. Shit!

It rains all day long. We are marching in the rain, searching vehicles in the rain, digging foxholes in the rain, standing guard in the rain, and even eating in the rain. This day is not a good day.

Laying in the wet grass at Ft. Lewis on perimeter defense

We've been told that this lane training will go on for five days. You have got to be kidding me. Five days in the rain and cold of Washington playing at war. Fuck!

After we get back my gear, and everyone else's, is laid out all over the floor trying to get dry. SNAFU! Situation normal, all fucked up!

Thursday / 3-6-2003

What a fucked up day! This is one of the worst days I've ever spent in the Army. I got up at 0500. I had to draw the 50 cal again because of our fuck-ass platoon sergeant and our platoon lieutenant. Again, the other platoons going with us out to the field don't have to bring theirs, but 3rd platoon does. God Damn it!

—

I get to the field and my battle buddy and I are told to hump the 50 cal to the farthest distance to a foxhole on the perimeter. Then we are told to set the Ma-Duce up and dig the foxhole so that we can walk completely around it. It's pouring rain, I'm standing in mud and water up to my ankles, and I've got to dig a bigger hole. Holy shit! My battle buddy and I dug for six hours and still didn't have the foxhole done completely the way our asshole instructors wanted it. What the fuck? Am I a truck driver or a fucking infantry grunt? This is bullshit! There was even a period of time where sleet was coming down on top of us instead of the usual rain.

I'm told we will have to bring the 50 cal out with us again tomorrow. Christ, this is getting ridiculous. Everyone is pissed off unless they are too stupid to know better. I know I am pissed.

Friday / 3-7-2003

Today was another shitty day. It was the same schedule of standing in a foxhole around the 50 cal. At least we didn't have to dig any more today. It didn't rain as much today but it did hail on us three times. I just laid in the foxhole all day trying to stay dry, which was fucking impossible. I even got into an argument with another soldier over a fucking shovel. What the fuck was that all about? I think I'm losing it already.

At the end of the day as we were loading up into the cattle cars to take us back to the barracks, we were told to "stand-fast." That means stop moving and wait because they have something else to fuck with you about. Seems there is a missing pair of gloves that are used to handle barbed wire. These are special gloves and apparently the Army wants them back. So, we have to form one long line and walk through the entire area of operations (AO) to look for them. Now we've been outside all day. We're all tired, sick, cold, soaked, and thoroughly pissed off and of course, no one finds the gloves. So we stand in formation again in the rain and wait for the cattle cars to come back because it seems some soldiers got on them before the rest of us were stopped. I am so mad I can't see straight but there is nothing I can do about any of this bullshit.

The one good thing about today is that I am so tired that I actually sleep through the night despite still being sick. That was a nice change.

Latest rumor before I fall asleep among all the wet gear is we're headed back to Camp Roberts on the 12th and in Kuwait by April 4th. We'll see.

Saturday / 3-8-2003

I'm back in the field again. Nothing different to write about. It rained all day and it's cold and muddy and I'm miserable. My clothes are soaked through and stained with mud as well as my hands. I'm tired beyond belief and could really use some niceness in my life right about now.

Sunday / 3-9-2003

It's the last day in the field and I can't wait for this day to end. It rained even harder today that it has for any of the past few days. I was soaked through by 0900. My clothes just can't take anymore water and mud.

At the end of the day we had to walk through the AO and make sure all the foxholes were filled back in and all the sandbags were emptied. We also had to pick up anything that didn't belong out there. There were about three hundred of us walking through the mud and rain with our heads down and boots sticking with every step. I don't think I can feel any worse than I do right now.

It's 1600 and we are all standing in formation waiting for the cattle cars to come and pick us up and take us out of this hellhole. As we stand there the rain stops and the sun peaks out. The most common remark is something like, "You've got to be shitting me!" After spending five days in the rain, wind, sleet, and cold, just as we are about to walk out of the woods on the last day of field training, the fucking sun comes out. Unfuckingbelievable!

Tonight's rumor is that we will be going to a Camp Chicago in Kuwait. I'm too tired to give a shit.

I have to clean all my gear and clothes as best I can and let them dry out. Again, everything is everywhere in the barracks. Gear draped over foot lockers, off the doors of our clothes lockers, clothes hanging from the ends of the bunks, and everyone is just exhausted. I'm glad this part of training is over.

Monday / 3-10-2003

We spend the day cleaning our weapons and gear. After five days in rain and mud everything is a mess. At least we are warm and sitting in the barracks able to shoot-the-shit while we clean.

We are not getting any down time (time to ourselves). We are going to leave tomorrow for Camp Roberts in California. We are suppose to be leaving early, too. So, we have to have our duffel bags packed and be ready to go by the time it's lights out tonight. Since I've picked up even more shit here in Ft. Lewis I have no fucking idea how I'm going to get everything in the two duffel bags that I could barely pack on the trip up here. This should be interesting.

This evening I got to lay around and it felt good. It is a relief that the five days in the field are over with. I sure as hell don't want to do that again. I'm pissed off that we don't get any down time, though. That sucks!

I took a quick trip to the PX and bought some postcards with pictures of the 50 cal on them. I need a few post cards to remind myself of what the hell it is I did here in Ft. Lewis.

I go to bed early and don't even bother taking my uniform off. I do take the boots off to rest the feet. If we are getting up as early as they are hinting at, it doesn't make sense to undress and pretend I'm going to get a good night's sleep. I throw the one blanket I have over me and crash.

Tuesday / 3-11-2003

Holy shit! They weren't kidding when they said we were going to get up early. They woke our asses up at 0230. I am really happy that I didn't bother to undress last night as I sit up, rub my eyes, cuss for a few minutes, and put my boots on. I'm ready to go.

We load up on the buses at 0430. I can barely see because my eyes are burning from a lack of sleep. Good thing it's dark outside because there is nothing to see anyway.

We fly back to California, ride on another bus, and get to Camp Roberts. It feels good to be back in the sunshine and warmer weather.

We don't have to do anything once we unload our gear and grab our bunks again. So, I take off for the small PX they have here. It's not much but it's all we have and I could use some snacks and a hot dog.

I'm getting pretty close to a guy I'll call M. He's a teacher from up around Sacramento and he's a very smart and funny guy. He is also the one guy who seems to have a brain in his head around here. He knows his shit about the trucks, too. It's good to have one friend who doesn't drive me nuts or who isn't a drunk or who is just so stupid that I want to crush their face.

I called my Ma today and she said something that made me laugh out loud. I told her we were still going overseas and she said, "Do they know how old you are?" I just lost it and bent over with laughter. My Ma is pretty funny and she doesn't even know she's making a joke. I didn't have the heart to tell her that the Army really doesn't give a shit how old you are, they need bodies. Besides, I signed the paper and collected the paycheck for all these years. I guess I have nothing to complain about. But, I will!

I'm sitting on a bench outside the PX and enjoying the warm weather. It's nice to just take some time for myself. It starts all over again tomorrow. Yippee!

Wednesday / 3-12-2003

We finally had an easy day today. We just sat around in the barracks and pretended to listen to the CTT classes. The hardest part of this day was staying awake. After the past few days we went through at Ft. Lewis we are all a little drained.

The sun is out and it's warm and everyone is happy about that. I went to the PX for lunch. If I can help it I don't go to the mess hall at all anymore because the food is so bad. Even breakfast sucks, but there is nothing else open on base at that time so, I go.

We were released at 1600. The rest of the day was spent talking, sleeping, reading, writing, and watching DVDs. It seems that everyone has their own laptop computer and DVDs up the ass to watch. I ordered a small DVD player from the PX today so I can watch my own movies. It's hard to watch a movie with about ten guys all trying to get their heads in front of one computer. If you are a little off to the side the picture isn't very clear.

The latest rumor is that we could get some days off soon. I don't know why they don't release us to spend some time with our families before we go to Iraq.

I went on line for awhile and checked the emails. Not much there. It's a warm beautiful night and I'm happy about that.

Thursday / 3-13-2003

Another day of classes. It's total bullshit and I can tell they don't have anything specific for us to do so they are just bidding their time with this crap.

I got off at 1600 again today and went to the laundry mat. The weather is cooler today but still one hundred percent better than Ft. Lewis in Washington. We are suppose to have some more field training next week and it sounds like a lot of bullshit headed our way again. We're are to spend four hours a day in our MOPP suits (chemical uniform and mask), sleep in tents at night, and play war games. I thought we just did that shit.

I've been writing a lot of letters but I haven't gotten any mail yet. I hope the mail catches up with us soon.

More bullshit to follow.

Friday / 3-14-2003

Another wasted day. We were up at 0530, went to chow at 0600, and classes at 0800. I don't think I can listen to another asshole talk about some subject that he is reading from a fucking manual for much longer. These classes are a complete waste of time.

After a while we went out to a spot near the barracks where there is some open space. They have a HET parked and we are suppose to put a camouflaged netting over it. Are you fucking kidding me? First of all, the cammo netting is for the forest and is mostly green. If I remember my geography books from school the desert is fucking brown. And, do they really think we'll be putting a cammo net on our trucks after driving all day in Iraq? I don't get the Army. Sometimes they have no common sense. We put the netting up twice and then called it a day. At least I wasn't in some boring-ass CTT class all day.

I bought my DVD player today. Now I can watch my own videos on my chest as I lay in bed. This DVD player is too small for more than one person to watch unless they put their cheek next to mine, which isn't going to happen.

We're just wasting our time until Monday. It's pure bullshit! We should be with our families. I miss my kids.

Saturday / 3-15-2003

Nothing much happening today. We had more CTT classes in the morning and practiced loading a Hummer on a HET in the afternoon. Our platoon, the 3rd, is having a barbecue tonight. I'm looking forward to food that has some fucking taste for a change, unlike what we get in the mess hall.

I talked with both my daughters today. They are fine. A few complaints here and there, but all in all, I'm happy they aren't killing each other as they never have gotten along very well. I love my kids.

Sunday / 3-16-2003

Not much to do today. We just sat around, went to the PX, and did nothing.

Everyone is starting to gear up for tomorrow so we got busy about 1900 until 2200. You'd think they would of started this a little earlier today, but like always, idiots are in charge. I had no time for a DVD tonight but I did get to drive a round in a HET for a short distance.

Monday / 3-17-2003

And so it begins. We got up at 0400 and formation was at 0430. A lot of the guys were late getting to formation so we got royally chewed out by Top (First Sergeant). After getting reamed we drove out to a place they call, "Sherwood Forest." I guess it's suppose to be named after Robin Hood and his Merry Men, but none of us are very merry right now and we sure as shit don't have a Robin Hood with us. This is the forest area where you do your field training at Camp Roberts in California.

When we first got there we were acting as if we were entering a hostile area so we had to lay down in the wet fucking grass and pretend we were putting up a defensive line.

After entering the area we set up our perimeter. My battle-buddy and I set up the 50 cal at the front entrance and waited. We waited there for eleven hours. I'm pretty sure once we got there no one gave a shit to replace us or more likely, they just forgot about us. This actually turned out to be a good thing as we didn't do shit all day except sit in the foxhole and shoot the shit and relax. Not a bad day in the California sun. After a while we actually took turns taking naps in the grass.

We finally were allowed to go back to the tent about 2100. As I was walking back to our tent in the dark (when in the field you have to have "light discipline" which means no white lights, only the red lens on your flash light) I stepped into a hole and twisted my knee. It hurts a little and my battle buddy got a real good laugh out of it. As we walked into the tent almost every other guy in our platoon was already in their sleeping bag racked out. Figures. They did forget about us. Fucking Army! So, here we are laying shoulder to shoulder in our sleeping bags on the ground. After spending the entire day on perimeter and doing infantry crap I was happy to be going to sleep.

Tuesday / 3-18-2003

I went to sick call for my knee that is still hurting. It was strange standing in the CQ tent (Charge of Quarters or headquarters tent). Everyone was getting geared up for the day, people walking here and there, radios squawking, and just a bunch of activity everywhere, and I was just standing there waiting for someone to take me out of the field. We have no hospital or infirmary on the camp so we have to be driven into the local town of Paso Robles to a clinic. I leave my weapon and gear behind and climb into a Hummer to head for camp. Once I get to the camp I get on a Army bus and am driven into town. I am sent to the local hospital so they can x-ray my knee. I get a young doctor who is obviously anti-military and his attitude shows. I want to rip his fucking head off, but this isn't the place or time. His verdict is to "take it easy on that knee." Fucking brilliant! I try to explain that it's impossible to "take it easy on that knee" when you are in the woods playing war games, but it doesn't get through to his thick fucking skull. So, I'm returned to the field with no light duty. I am pissed off beyond belief!

The bus lets us off at a local store where I buy a DVD and some other junk that I'll probably never use. It was great to see actual people walking around, especially the women. I love women!

As I come back to the field and put my gear back on and grab my weapon my platoon sergeant thanks me for coming back. I didn't tell him I had no fucking choice. Most of my platoon is on the perimeter pulling guard duty so I just crawl into my sleeping bag and nod off.

Wednesday / 3-19-2003

We are still playing war games. We're driving our trucks out in the woods and getting ambushed along the way. We always stop, get gassed, and get reamed out by our evaluators who think we can't do anything right (are they right)? Everyone is frustrated and tired and angry. It's all bullshit! We are playing the 11B (infantry) game but we have to drive a truck, too. Will we be doing all of this shit over in Iraq? I hope not. I hope there is the actual infantry to do all this running around after bad guys shit. I'm just suppose to drive a truck.

We're getting up at 0400 every day out here and getting back after dark. Everyone is dead on their feet. Sick call is skyrocketing. Some guys are trying anything and everything they can think of to get out of this bullshit. I don't blame them. I feel like quitting, too.

After being up late last night fighting off a breech in our perimeter our platoon sergeant told us we could sleep an extra hour. It's pitch black inside the tent and it's 0400 and we are all happy for the extra hour of sleep ahead of us. All of a sudden our platoon asshole speaks up. He starts his usual stammering and mumbling. Something like, "Well . . . well . . . what about 3rd platoon . . . well . . . what are we suppose to do? . . . uh, what about 3rd platoon? . . . uh" So, after our platoon sergeant had told us we could sleep a little longer gets pissed off and yells at us to "Get your asses up if you want to question me." Now we're getting up getting our gear on with everyone else and I'm laying next to this asshole. I start calling him every name in the book and telling him how fucking stupid he is. I want to jump on top of him and start beating his fucking head in. What a dumb ass! Some of these guys are so stupid I wonder how they learned how to hold a fork in order to feed themselves. Asshole!

Thursday / 3-20-2003

Today we drove our trucks over to a parking lot where they had some vehicles outside for us to practice loading up. It's easy to load a vehicle when it can drive up the ramp onto our trailer, but if the vehicle is disabled, then it's a real bitch. We have to winch it onto the trailer. That means that we have to back the truck up in front of the tracked vehicle and then pull this really heavy-duty steel cable back to the broken down tank. After you connect the cable to the tank then you have to go to a platform on the back of the trailer that controls the cable and start pulling the vehicle. It's a slow process because you have keep the tracks lined up with the ramps leading to the trailer and it just doesn't go very fast.

After all, you're pulling up to seventy tons with this cable. You stand behind this wire screen that is there in case the cable breaks and comes whipping back at you. If this cable breaks and comes whipping back at me I will be Swiss cheese as this screen is not going to stop this big ass cable. I just can't stop thinking of that cable coming back at me as I winch the tank up. I'm such a chicken-shit when it comes to stuff like this because my mind won't leave me alone. I guess these dumb asses who never think of this stuff are blessed because they are so stupid this stuff never enters their minds. I did everything like I was suppose to and I understand the process. At least I learned something today.

I'm sitting on the neck of the trailer pretending to pull as hard as I can
while we winch a tracked Bradley vehicle onto a HET

As we got done winching the tracked vehicles onto our trucks we then were suppose to be under attack by what the Army calls "OPFOR." This stands for "Opposition Forces" which means they are the bad guys. We end up standing in the street around the fenced yard that our trucks are in. We are standing there with our weapons and battle-rattle on watching a bunch of civilians sitting on the porches of barracks in front of us. They aren't doing shit but sitting there and talking. We aren't doing shit but standing and staring at them with our M-16s in our hands. It's stupid! Luckily there is one young woman who is attractive so I just stare at her and dream. At least it helped me pass the time doing nothing.

We didn't get done today until late. I guess the war games are winding down because of all the complaints that our evaluators are getting. Tonight we are told that we can sleep from 2000 to 0530. That would be the first full night's sleep in a while and I could use it. Before we are allowed to head for the field to sleep in the tents on the ground again, I sneak away and walk to our barracks about one mile away. I go straight to the showers and clean myself off as I haven't showered in a few days. It was worth the risk! I feel a little human again.

Friday / 3-21-2003

Today we are taking a convoy to another base close by called Hunter-Leggett. We loaded up our trucks with some tracked vehicles and moved out ahead of schedule. Of course, we are in our battle-rattle with weapons as this is a tactical convoy.

Posing at Camp Roberts, California

On the way there we were ambushed by our evaluators, as usual. We stopped the convoy and got out and laid in the grass alongside our trucks. As I was laying in the grass the signal came out for "gas." It's suppose to be banging on metal, or the call of "gas" but in our long convoys, we listen for three beeps of a truck horn. I masked up and laid there with my M-16 pointed outward loaded with a clip of blanks (rounds that make the noise like a round but do not have a bullet). I noticed a couple of "bad guys" in a grove of trees near my truck. They are firing their weapons and aiming at a couple trucks behind mine. I decided to attack them. I started crawling in the grass toward their position. As I got closer I fired my rifle at them. They didn't seem to hear my firing over their own firing. So, I figured I had to get closer to get their attention. I crawled up to about twenty feet and leaned against a tree and opened up on automatic. That got their attention but they just looked at me and then started shooting at me. Now, if I got the draw on them, shouldn't they be dead? How can they continue to shoot at me if I already wiped their asses out? It's the same old "cowboys and Indians" I used to play as a kid. "Bang, bang. You're dead!" And then the other person yells, "No, I'm not. Bang, bang. You're dead." and so on and so on. Now, the military does have a system set up where you can wear sensors on your helmet and your web gear that when a laser beam strikes it you will beep. You have to have a special little box on the end of your rifle that emit's the ray when your rifle fires, but we weren't wearing them today. After the battle was over I leaned on the tree and ripped my mask off my face as I was sweating like crazy. I hate wearing that fucking mask because I get claustrophobic and hot as hell. As I laid against the tree close to passing out one of the evaluators came up to me and told me I did a good job reacting to the ambush. That is the first fucking compliment I have gotten during this entire activation from them. He told me that if it had been a real battle he would of put me in for a bronze star medal. I didn't have the heart to tell him that if it had been a real battle I'd probably be hiding under the truck with my pants soiled from shitting myself.

We drove to Hunter-Leggett and back after the ambush without much else happening. Although, our convoy did take a wrong turn and ended up driving about two hours out of our way getting back. We got back pretty late. My battle-buddy for the day fucked up the winching part of the day as well as hitting a cement barrier with the trailer. He also got the truck stuck in the grass earlier. All in all, a normal Army day. SNAFU!

Saturday / 3-22-2003

I got over ten letters in the mail yesterday. Finally, the mail has arrived. It was great reading all those letters and finding out about everyone back home.

I get to see my daughters today. I can't wait.

After they showed up we went to the local town, Paso Robles, and got a motel room. We went to the local movie theater and saw a really funny movie together. It was good to laugh again. We ate dinner, had fun all day, and I just felt great being with my kids again. They are very special to me.

Sunday / 3-23-2003

The local town of Paso Robles put on a huge picnic for our unit at the camp. It seems there was some guy on a local radio show who was complaining about seeing some of us in the town drinking beer. I don't know what the hell he was upset about, but the local townspeople went nuts on him calling the station back and supporting us. So, the town took up collections and put on a barbecue with all kinds of food including an American flag made out of hundreds of cupcakes. It was a great day and the food was perfect! Oh yeah, and there was all the free beer we could drink at that picnic. Thank you America and the people of Paso Robles. The local TV reporters were there and I heard later that we made the TV, but I didn't see it. It was a pretty special day for all of us and our families.

Monday / 3-24-2003

After spending last night in Paso Robles with the girls, it was hard saying good-bye this morning. Not knowing if I'll see them again before I leave for Iraq is very hard on both the girls and myself. There were a few tears this morning.

It was a pretty easy day for us. My battle-buddy and I drove a HET to a wash rack. We just sat in the HET and did nothing but wait for our turn to wash our truck. I took a couple naps and read the newspaper.

The war in Iraq is not going well right now. G.I.s are dying. I'm glad we're back here. I know that sounds unpatriotic, but I'm a little scared of going to war. I don't care if we ever go. The war is dirty and nasty and I'd rather go home.

Back in the barracks I watched a couple DVDs on my player. I really love having my own personal DVD player. I get ready for bed, put a DVD in the player, prop my head up on my pillow, put the player on my chest, and with the earphones plugged in, I can disappear into a movie for a couple hours and leave this place. I don't hear the noise and people around me and I'm not in the Army for a while.

I got a bunch of letters from friends and school today. That always helps.

Thursday / 3-25-2003

Another easy day. I drove a HET to the wash rack again and did the same as yesterday. I napped, read the paper, and just sat in the cab of the truck talking with my battle-buddy. It takes so long to wash the trucks that I only had to take two all day. That's a lot of sitting and I enjoyed it.

One of the trucks had a little problem so we were told to wait for maintenance until they could fix the problem. They never showed up. After sitting around waiting for them until 2200 we drove the truck back to our company area, parked it, and I went into the orderly room (where our headquarters is) and asked them, "Does anyone know what the fuck is going on here?" I was pissed! I went to my barracks, didn't shower, didn't watch a movie, and just got into bed. I was too tired to deal with the stupidity anymore for today.

A letter I sent to my school / 3-25-2003

Hey Everyone,

I got a bunch of letters the other day from students and staff. Thank you very much. The bright spot of the day is when I get back to the barracks and there is mail on my bunk.

Since we've been back in CA we spent five days and nights in the woods practicing our skills. Perimeter defense, weapons training, convoy procedures during enemy contact, radio procedures, etc. We need to get our skill levels up before we go over to the sandbox (that's what we call Iraq, or simply, "the box"). Sleeping on the ground in the cold night without showers or hot chow is tough, but at least we're not in the war zone. I respect and admire the people who are over there in harm's way.

I got a chance to visit with my two daughters last week end. That was a great treat. It's hard saying good-bye again, though. The future is so uncertain that it's hard to remain sane and relaxed. The troops are in good spirits but anxious.

I still get up at 5 AM and start my day at 7 AM. Depending on what goes on during the day depends on when we get in. I got in at 9 PM last night, cleaned up, and passed out in the bunk. I can't believe I'm falling asleep before 10 PM.

My hands are rough and dirty. Not teacher hands anymore. The feet have healed and calloused up. My daughters think I've lost weight so I guess the changes aren't all bad.

I hope everyone at school is doing well and my class is hanging in there. I will write them a separate letter (principal, please read it first and make sure everything is OK).

I'm nervous about the future because of the news coming from the war but I am still dedicated to the cause and the United States.

Keep your letters coming because they are important to me and I appreciate the time you take to write them.

Joe

Wednesday / 3-26-2003

It was a hard day today. Our trucks are getting validated for overseas. That means that some inspectors will be looking over the trucks to make sure everything is ready for them to be shipped to Kuwait so they will be there waiting when we get there. That means we have to clean them. So, I spent the entire day shoveling the mud and washing the trucks at the wash rack. I am very sore.

I am ready to go home. The hell with this shit! I'm tired and sore and sick of being dicked with here. We are still suppose to be going overseas in a couple weeks to Iraq. I'm scared because the Iraqis are hitting convoys and that's what we'll be doing. I'd be happy to be home right now but it's not in my hands.

Thursday / 3-27-2003

We spent the whole day loading and unloading a Bradley Fighting Vehicle on a HET. We had to winch the damn thing on the trailer every time. I stood around most of the day trying to look like I was busy when really I was avoiding doing as much as I could. I'm sunburned and wind burned. I'm getting bloody noses every day now. I've already had three today.

I talked to my Ma today and my kids. It's always good to talk with them but hard, too. I try and not to talk about going to war but what the hell else am I suppose to talk about here? The weather?

They called a formation at 2000. We got in our NBC (nuclear, biological, and chemical uniforms). They are brand new, still in the package. That means we're really going over there. Goddamn it! Iraq, here I come!

Friday / 3-28-2003

It wasn't a bad day today. We had NBC training all morning. We practiced putting on our new chemical uniforms with the mask. They are much better than the old ones that we used to carry around for practice. They are desert camouflaged where the old ones were the forest green cammo. The only problem is they are still lined with charcoal and hot as fucking shit! I hate wearing them. I also have a problem that I can't let the Army know about. I'm extremely claustrophobic and I start to panic when I'm in this get-up. I was in the barracks putting all this shit on including the mask when after making sure the collar was all buttoned up and all the straps were secure, I had to rip the damn mask off. I can't do it. If a soldier is that claustrophobic then they are deemed "non-deployable." I just told the guy I was feeling a little ill and he let it go. I sure hope I never have to wear this shit for real in Iraq because I'll probably commit suicide by ripping the outfit off. "Gee, kids, your Dad died because he ripped his mask off in the middle of a chemical attack. Sorry." Yeah, that's going to go over real big.

There is a lot of new equipment pouring in to our area. They are unloading boxes and boxes of shit all over the place.

Large semi-trucks are coming and going with our HETs loaded on the back. There is a large crane here that loads the cab of our truck onto a semi, then the trailer goes on another semi. They are coming and going all day long. I'm told they are being driven to some port in Texas for the shipment overseas. We are definitely going to the 'box.' April 2nd is suppose to be our validation date, or the date where we qualify to leave for Iraq. Looks like we'll make it this time. Shit! I hope for the best!

Saturday / 3-29-2003

Today started out pretty easy. We had classes on convoy ambushes and what to do. Now, we didn't actually go on a convoy, we just talked about going on a convoy in enemy territory. Much easier than actually doing it. Besides, they are loading all our trucks and we don't have anything to drive anymore. I stood around in the sun and heat all day trying to pay attention to these classes but basically, lost the battle. I'm worn out and I need some downtime.

Our trucks are still being loaded onto semi trucks and heading out. It's quite an operation.

Our company is suppose to have a barbecue tonight. It's always fucking Mexican food. It'd be nice to have a fucking hamburger or a steak once in a while. I know this is California, but give me a fucking break.

Sunday / 3-30-2003

I was in the sun for most of the day. It's hot and we are all sunburned. I drove two HETs to the crane for loading today. Nothing much else to do now.

My battle-buddy and I are working to secure a tracked vehicle
on the HET trailer with chains. I am in the background.

I did some laundry this evening then walked over to the club for a beer and some pizza. Everyone gathers around the TV to watch the news about the war in Iraq. Every time they show something or someplace blown up in Iraq we all cheer. When they talk about American casualties we are quiet.

I'm tired, tired, tired . . .

Monday / 3-31-2003

This is the 3rd day in a row of loading our trucks for transportation to Iraq. Our platoon, 3rd platoon, always seems to get the shit details. I had to work with the crane today loading the trucks. It's actually interesting, but hard. There is a lot of pushing, lifting, and connecting of large cables in order to get the truck loaded on the semi. It's so hot we were allowed to take our blouses off (the Army, in it's infinite wisdom, calls the shirts we wear "blouses" which sounds really stupid to me, but hey, what the hell do I know)? Since I was in my t-shirt all day I really got sunburned on my arms and face. Ow!

I got some down time in the morning which was a nice change. I went back to the barracks and laid on my bunk for about an hour.

I had CQ (charge of quarters) from 1800-2100. I had to sit at a table in the headquarter building and answer the phone if it rang. I also sign people out when they have to leave the camp for any reason. Really, there is nothing to do, but I hate sitting in the middle of where all the officers are. They are sitting at their desks a few feet away and I am trying to be as invisible as possible. The only good part about CQ here is that when they talk about something that effects me, I can hear the information. The latest scuttlebutt is we are leaving on the 9th of April to Kuwait.

We had two heat casualties today that had to be taken to the local hospital. It's been really hot here lately and the guys are having trouble. I wonder how we'll do in the real desert of Iraq? Will we all faint?

I have to get up at 0400 tomorrow for more war games. Great! I can't wait. I hope I get to see my kids again soon. The Army is crap and I'm tired of all this bullshit. No DVD for me tonight, just sleep.

Tuesday / 4-1-2003

We're up at 0400 to prepare for our tactical move to the field. I was on the advanced party to the AO (that means I went in with the first small group to secure the area that we will be operating in). Of course, we're back in Sherwood Forest and the same place we played war the last time we went to the field. We went in with our gas masks on and had to wear them for forty minutes while we set up our perimeter. I hate wearing that fucking gas mask. It's uncomfortable, hot, and you can't see shit when you're wearing it. All you can hear is your own heavy breathing. Every time someone tries to tell you something it sounds like they have a mouth full of marbles and I never know what the hell they are saying.

After we set up the perimeter the rest of the company came driving in like they were on a holiday. It was a pretty big let down after what we had to go through to secure the perimeter. After everyone got settled down we had classes all morning. I was assigned to listen to a radio in a Hummer and to answer it if any radio traffic came through. After sitting there for over an hour and not hearing anything, some guy came over and told me I had the radio on the wrong frequency so I wouldn't of heard any of the shit I was suppose to. I was secretly happy that I fucked up because it kept me from having to do anything for that hour. I did pretend that I was really upset and angry that I didn't get to monitor the radio chatter.

Lunch was a relaxed time. We all just laid around in the grass, ate our shitty MREs (called "Meals Ready to Eat" that come in a bag for eating in the field). We managed to waste the rest of the day and got back in the barracks at 1630.

I showered, put a clean uniform on, and headed for the club for some pizza after the 1800 formation.

I had my daughter, Jennie, buy a new car for me. I needed one and she did a great job buying it for me. Actually, she'll be using it until I come home again, so it's really for her to get to college and work. I talked to her on the phone and she sounded all right. I didn't get a chance to talk to Christie as she wasn't home when I called. I haven't talked with her for a while. I hope we get some time off soon.

I was walking with a friend of mine this evening and we saw a rainbow in the sky. It was a really nice view as the clouds were dark, the sun was shinning, and the rainbow was arched across the sky with the flag flying underneath it. My friend and I took it as a sign that everything will be fine in the future. Is that how fucked up I really am that seeing a rainbow makes my future safe? I must be desperate.

Wednesday / 4-2-2003

Today was a pretty full day and I actually had some fun. First, we did a lot of training in classes again. It was all outside. We covered map reading, weapons, anti-tank weapons, M-249 SAW (squad automatic weapon), Mark-19 (grenade launcher), and a few other items.

The best part of the day was our training in a computer room that was set up for us to have a practice battle. In the room is a row of stations that can hold up to about ten soldiers. We put our M-16s down and are assigned a spot with a rifle that is connected to the computer system. It's the same weight and shape of a real M-16 so it's like shooting the real thing. In front of our positions there is a large screen like in a movie theater. After an instructor explains how to use the system we are told that we will be looking at a scene on the screen. Who ever was chosen to be the team leader assigns people their field of fire and the screen comes alive. My situation is that we are in a defensive posture and enemy contact is expected. As I am watching my field of responsibility on the screen I begin to see people sneaking through the trees. Our line opens fire on the targets on the screen. I aim and shoot and repeat as long as we are being attacked. At the end of the exercise the instructor punches up the computer and it tells us our scores of how many hits we had, even kills. I didn't hit one enemy target. I was so deflated. I thought I had killed all of the bad guys I had aimed at on the screen. I was really embarrassed. I had to wait outside while I hoped to get back in there and redeem myself but I never got another chance. All in all, I hope a bunch of bad guys trying to kill me never come at me because apparently I won't be able to shoot any of them and I'll die. Fuck!

I'm going home Friday and I can't wait. The Army is still dicking with us. We are getting up at 0530 for PT (physical training). We are all so beat up I'm not sure how much this running in the morning is going to help, but that's what we'll be doing. I think this is a big mistake.

I hope I get laid this week end.

Thursday / 4-3-2003

We had classes all day today. Boring as hell. I was so bored that I wrote letters during the classes. After a while we all had to clean our gas masks, so we sat around and shot the shit with each other while cleaning.

We've had to wear our flak vest for three days now. It's heavy but not too bad.

Our instructors are telling us that we are not qualified to go overseas yet and haven't earned our validation. Yikes! What the hell did we do wrong now?

I went to the club for beer and pizza and then came back to the barracks. I sacked out at 2100.

My ride is set up for tomorrow to go home. I can't wait and I have a new car to drive. Whee!

Letter to school / 4-3-2003

Hi,

Thanks for the letters. It was nice to hear from you. I am still in California, but will be leaving for Iraq in a couple weeks.

We're learning a lot of things to help us when we get overseas. There is a lot to learn, so this teacher is paying attention.

During the final two weeks we will practice some of the things we have learned. We need to be ready as soon as we get there.

Mail is a great treat here. Your letters were fun to read and put a smile on my face. So, again, thanks for taking the time to write.

We have loaded up all our trucks and they are on their way to Texas. In Texas they will be loaded on a ship. It will take 2-3 weeks for them to get to Kuwait. We will meet them over there.

Keep in touch. Your letters are very important to me.

Mr. Berlin

Friday / 4-4-2003

We got up at 0445 today. PT is at 0530. I must be losing weight and getting in better shape because I made the 1.5 mile run today. I haven't run any distance in years.

After PT we got to go back to the barracks and clean up. Then we sat around the rest of the morning waiting for our 1300 formation. What a fucking waste of time. We could of just gotten up today and left, but the fucking Army had to dick with us until the afternoon. No sense letting us go visit our families early when they can make us sit around for a few hours for no fucking reason.

The guy who rented our car is a total alcoholic. We went into Paso Robles to rent the car and this fucker is drinking before we even sign that damn thing out. I can't wait for this fucking ride. I'm going to be killed in a drunk driver accident on my way home before I ever ship out to the war in Iraq. Perfect!

I made it home and it feels good. The girls and I rented a movie and we're just going to sit around, watch TV, and enjoy each other's company. It's a little weird in that it feels strange to be home right now. Have I been gone that long? Is the Army getting into my brain that much? I'm suppose to feel normal at home, not Camp Roberts, California. Very weird!

Saturday / 4-5-2003

I had to take my new car back to the dealer today for a little "attitude adjustment." Seems that my daughter was driving the new car and someone had signaled something was wrong with her rear tire. She stopped and had to change the tire. Apparently she scratched the paint and bent a part of the car's underside trying to jack the car up. I had told her to take it back to the dealer and have them fix it as the car was brand new and shouldn't of had a problem in the first place. Well, I guess the sight of a small young lady gave the people at the car dealership the courage to tell her, "No." So, I went down there and explained my situation and told them of this office the Army has called the JAG which stands for the Judge Advocate General. This is the place that takes care of legal problems in the Army and has a lot of clout. As soon as I mentioned that I would get in contact with the JAG office this guy changed his story and had the car fixed at his expense. My argument was that when my daughter picked the car up the salesman never went over the operation of the car including changing a tire. I guess these people didn't want to "Support the troops" unless they had to. Bastards!

After that we just ran some errands around town and went out to eat. It was a good day because I got to spend time with my daughters.

Sunday / 4-6-2003

I had breakfast with the girls and then we walked to the beach. I just sat with the girls until it was time to go at 7 PM. Of course, the alcoholic driver of ours was late picking me up and reeked of booze, so I was pissed as I got into the car to start the drive back to camp. We got back at 2300 and I fell asleep right away.

Monday / 4-7-2003

We got up at 0430, did our PT at 0530, and the pain came at 0550. Fuck! It hurts to do exercise and run after sitting on my ass for the past two days eating and doing nothing.

We had classes in the barracks all day today and it was fucking boring. How many times can we waste our time going over the same shit that no one cares about anyway?

I got a letter from the teachers that I used to work with back in Michigan before my move to California. It was very nice and made me miss that life back there for awhile. I wrote a ton of letters myself tonight.

The news says that Saddam was killed today. I hope so. We're getting closer to leaving but they still won't tell us anything. I hate not knowing. Let's just get the hell over there.

Tuesday / 4-8-2003

We got up at 0430 again. Today we had to do PT in the wet grass. It's not very comfortable being in your shorts and shirts and laying in wet grass. When you do your crunches on your back there is no way to stay dry. We look like a mess and feel worse. I'm fucking miserable!

Now I know they don't know what to do with us. They took us on a 3-4 mile field march. We took our weapons and wore our battle-rattle. Then we pretended we were walking on a patrol in enemy territory. Did I join the infantry and someone forgot to tell me? What the fuck! It was a really hot, sweaty day for me. Wearing that flak vest all day in the sun was fucking brutal. And then something happened about halfway through the march that surprised me. I actually started enjoying myself. It was surprisingly fun doing the 11B (11 Bravo or infantry). I haven't done anything like this since basic training in 1969.

I'm headed into town to see a movie and get some food. The only problem is there is no transportation so I guess that's out. It sucks having to depend on a military bus to take us anywhere because most of the time we can't find the fucking driver. He's probably in town himself eating and hiding while we stand around waiting for him to show up. What a prick!

I'm going on sick call tomorrow because I'm running out of my blood pressure medicine. I need to stock up before we are deployed overseas. Who knows the next time I'll be able to get my meds?

The company is suppose to do NBC training tomorrow so I am really glad I'm going into town on sick call. I hate that shit!

Wednesday / 4-9-2003

I went into Paso Robles today on sick call. It was an easy day for me and I enjoyed it. I still have blood pressure that is too high but I'm not worried. I really don't see how I'm suppose to control my blood pressure when I'm not getting good sleep, I'm eating lousy food every day, I'm being dicked with all day and every day, and I have the treat of going to war and getting killed. How the hell is that suppose to calm me?

The doctor wanted me to go on some water pills to help control my blood pressure. I tried telling him that I'm going to a fucking desert and all I'm being told is to drink as much water as I can when I get there and this prick wants me to take a pill that will drain the water out of me? What a fucknut! I took the pills but have no intention of taking them.

When I came back from sick call I was walking back to the barracks and could see the guys outside wearing their MOPP 4 gear (charcoal lined pants, shirts, rubber boots, rubber gloves, and mask). They were carrying some guy on a litter and looked abso-fucking-ultly miserable. I was so happy that I had not had to do that shit today I almost wet myself.

Later on I watched a video with the guys in the barracks. We sat around on a couple bunks and some folding chairs we had and watched a movie about a bunch of guys who do weird shit like lighting fireworks off in their ass, and hitting themselves in the nuts. Put a room full of Army guys in a group, put beer into them, and have them watch a dumbass movie like this, and you have some real fun. We laughed our asses off and drank a lot of beer.

Thursday / 4-10-2003

We started the day with a road march and then set up a defensive perimeter. While on the perimeter we were attacked by our evaluators. I shot two of their guys and then they killed my squad with a grenade. The fucking Army is like a bunch of kids sometimes. We didn't have our electronic gear that lets you record hits when you are having a practice battle, so it's like the old days where you fire your blanks and yell, "I got you!" Then the other guy, or guys, keeps running and hides and shoots back at you and yells, "No, you didn't. I got you!" And that keeps on going and going until you get so frustrated that you just don't give a shit anymore. That's how today's battle went. What a fucking joke!

The road march at Camp Roberts, California. I'm in the front

Fucking Army! We were told we would get a two day pass this coming week end and now they are cancelling it. Motherfuckers! I am so pissed. I'm going to go on sick call tomorrow to spite them. Fuck those assholes, I'm not doing shit! Fuckers!

Friday / 4-11-2003

The Army is fucking nuts! They changed their minds again (as if they actually have one). They are giving us the week end off. I'm glad but sick of how they dick with us all the time. I ended up going on sick call because I had to pick up my meds for the deployment. I got three meds and two of them are no good. The two meds that are worthless are suppose to help with my blood pressure by dehydrating me. Fucking idiots! I keep telling them I'm going to the desert where I will need a shitload of water, but they want me to get rid of the water in my body. These docs are stupid!

When I got back the guys were still on their road march so I went and did my laundry. I'm showered and looking for something to do. The club?

Saturday / 4-12-2003

I left camp at noon and got home around 3 PM. I watched my favorite hockey team lose the second game of the series to a fucking west coast team. I fell asleep in my rocker. That was nice. I'm so tired that I actually went to bed at 9:30 PM.

Sunday / 4-13-2003

I went to the movies with my girls today. While we were in the theater the fire alarm went off. We all had to exit the building. We ended up getting a free pass to another movie and then we were let back into the building to finish the one we were watching. Not a bad deal.

Monday / 4-14-2003

I bought some boots to wear in the desert today. According to the TV the war is over. I sure hope so. My girls and I went back to the movies today with that free pass that we got yesterday. Our neighbor female friend came along with us and yes, if I could, I would. I watched my hockey team lose to the west coast team again today. They are now down three games to none in their play off series and I fear they are toast. Yikes! I went to bed at midnight.

Tuesday / 4-15-2003

I got up at 0500 and of course the guys were late picking me up for the ride back to camp. We just drove in as the 1000 formation was forming. That was close.

We're just sitting in the barracks now with nothing to do. Everyone thinks we'll be going home soon.

Some of us went to the computer firing range to do something fun. I got to play several situations and it was fun. I finally got a few "kills" and decided that I'm ready to go to Iraq and shoot some fucking Iraqis.

A buddy of mine and me went to Paso Robles and decided to stay in a motel for the night instead of sleeping in the barracks again (we each got our own rooms, thank you). We ate some great barbecued ribs and then I spent the evening watching TV and wishing I had a woman with me.

The latest rumors are that we are now going home. I'm tired of not knowing. I wish they'd tell us one way or another.

Wednesday / 4-16-2003

Today we drove out to the field to practice ambushes. Each platoon gets to ambush another platoon. It's really fucked up. We are told the route that the platoon is going to come down and we get so much time to set up the ambush.

We were ambushed by 1st platoon first. As we were driving our Hummers and pick-ups down the dirt road there were some guys in the road so we stopped. That was our first mistake. As we were stopped in the road wondering if we should just shoot these guys or what the snipers opened up on us from the side and front. In the great scheme of things, I killed one of their snipers and one of them killed me. All in all, an even trade in our pretend war.

Next, we got to ambush the 4th platoon. I took off my Army blouse and put my gas mask hood on my head to look like an Iraqi. The plan was for me to stand in the road and get their convoy to stop like ours did so we could get them in the kill zone. So, I stood there like an idiot and waited for the convoy to show up. It did and I started babbling a bunch of nonsense and waving at them. They wouldn't let me get close to them so I got as close as I thought I could and threw a pretend grenade that I had hidden behind my water bottle at them. My grenade fell short and they allowed me to wound one soldier. But, they lit me up and sent me to my 96 virgins (killed). We didn't get the 4th platoon in the kill zone but we did all right. I had the guys take a picture of me pretending to be an Iraqi because no one would believe me if I tried to tell them what I did that day. I also had someone take a picture of me pretending to be on a shitter that was destroyed. I had a couple guys standing around me with their rifles pointed out like they were guarding me while I took a shit. Very funny. I can't wait to see how that one turns out.

I'm playing "Hagi" with my gas mask hood on my head.

Saturday / 4-19-2003

We practiced loading a M1 Abrams tank on a HET today. It was hot, sweaty, hard work. Climbing all over the trailer and the tank, securing the vehicle with chains, and everything else involved with winching a 70 ton tank onto our HET is hard, physical work. My knee is fucked up and hurting. In the afternoon we took the cab of a HET out into the woods and went trail riding. Each driver tried to hit the biggest water puddle or the biggest rut to bounce everyone around. I hit a pretty big rut and actually knocked a couple guys helmets into the roof. It's a good thing we were wearing our helmets or it would have been a real pain in the ass to come up with a story why a bunch of us had head injuries. We were actually laughing like a bunch of idiots. Big splashes and big bumps. It was great!

Sunday / 4-20-2003

It's Easter. Big fucking deal. At least we don't have to work today. A friend and me went into Paso Robles to spend the day and get rooms in the motel. Anything to get away from the camp and the Army life style.

I had to come back into camp from 1100-1500 for CQ. I put a DVD on my player to watch while we were in the headquarters because there was no one around, being Easter and all. Then back to the motel for some alone time and quiet.

Monday / 4-21-2003

I went back on sick call today because my knee is really starting to bother me. I had to be ready to go into Paso Robles for sick call at 0515 because the rest of the company was up and going to PT at that time. I didn't sleep well at all last night even though I was in a motel room. My knee is just hurting all the time now.

The Doctor wants me to get a MRI on my knee to find out what's going on. Finally.

I went back to camp and since the guys were out training I went and did my laundry. A couple of other guys from the company were there in the laundry mat. We sat around and bullshitted while we cleaned our clothes.

Back at the barracks I just sat around and talked with some of the guys. Our Lieutenant was there. He's cool, but a little weird. I read some mail. I got a nice card from the people at my school. Funny, they think I'm already in Iraq. I watched part of a DVD in my bunk but couldn't finish it. I'm just too tired.

I got up five times to piss this night. Unbelievable!

Tuesday / 4-22-2003

I went on sick call again today. I just sat in the doctor's office from 0900 until 1630. The ladies in the office were very nice, but there wasn't a lot to do sitting there for so fucking long. The MRI took 45 minutes and I have to come back for the results tomorrow.

After the time spent at the docs the bus stopped at the local shopping center. There is a girl inside one of the drug stores there that I'd flirted with yesterday. As I was standing outside waiting for the bus to load up to leave she came out and called me a "Butthead" for not coming in and talking to her. We've talked about going out and I guess I was suppose to talk to her about it today. I hope I get that cute ass.

I'm starting to feel left out after going on sick call for two days in a row now. The guys are cool about it so far, but it's like I've dropped off the face of the Earth for them lately.

We got a date for going overseas today. It's suppose to be May 2nd. We'll see. To me it's just another rumor and until it actually happens, I don't believe it.

Wednesday / 4-23-2003

It's my third day in a row for sick call. The results of my MRI state that I have "strained ligaments" in my right knee. It's nothing that will need surgery but it is validation that something is wrong with my knee. I went and tried to find that young prick of a doctor that told me to "take it easy" and sent me back into the field to finish the war games. I asked the nurse behind the counter if I could speak with him for a minute. I was going to tell him how big of an asshole he is and let him have it, but she said he wasn't there. I wonder if she could read my face and just decided to tell me that or if he was really not around. I really wanted to bite this prick's head off.

When the bus stopped at the shopping center I went in to talk with the girl that works there to set up the date for this coming week end. After getting a good look at her teeth, which were fucked up, I'm not sure I want to go out with her. She does have a nice ass, though. We're suppose to go out Friday night. I have no fucking idea how I'll get into town or what we'll do, but I'll be there.

I got back to the barracks and just hung out with the guys. I have a soft brace on my knee for now. I cleaned up and got into my bunk and tried to watch another DVD but couldn't finish it. I'm just too tired these days to stay up very late.

Thursday / 4-24-2003

I'm back with the guys today and it feels right. We got a 52 hour operation this week end so there goes the date I made for Friday night.

We went out in a convoy in the morning. It was a nice drive through the woods without any contact from the "bad guys." We drove out to the woods and set up a perimeter. I can tell we're getting better because we did what we had to in half the time it used to take us to set up a perimeter.

We finished up at noon and came back into camp. I got five hours of sleep in the barracks in the afternoon. Fantastic!

We went back out in the night for a short night operation. We got to use night vision goggles which was very cool. All we did was walk around in the dark and look at shit and go, "Wow! That's cool!" It's really something to look through those things. Everything looks green but it's pretty damn clear. The only problem is that you don't have any depth perception and I kept tripping in the ruts in the road. Still, very cool. There was no contact with OPFOR and I was back in bed by 2130.

Friday / 4-25-2003

I was up at 0600, went to eat breakfast, and then back in the barracks relaxing by 0830. This operation is going well. I'm getting a shitload of sleep. I've gotten more sleep in the past couple days then I did the past couple months. I spent the whole day doing nothing. I took two trips to the PX, one to the snack shop, read magazines, shot the shit with the guys, and just laid in my bunk the rest of the day.

I'm getting sick again. Fuck!

My daughters are coming up tomorrow. We're told this will be the last time we'll see our families. That is a really shitty thought. We are suppose to leave on the 28th which is in three days. It's weird to think that we are still going to Iraq after all this time we've been here fucking around.

Saturday / 4-26-2003

We had a formation at 0900. Our First Sergeant, or "Top," told us we'll be leaving in a few days and to get ready mentally. Fuck! How the hell do you mentally get ready to go halfway around the world to war? Good luck with that. At the end of the formation Top told us that we did not have passes to go anywhere. Are you fucking kidding me? My girls are suppose to be here at 1300 and we're not going to be released? Top is being a real asshole today. He's all pissed off because our families are coming, or already here, and he wants them gone. As he's telling us we can't see our families today, most of our families are standing right behind us. What the fuck is up his ass?

It's around noon and everyone's family is here and Top is pissed off. What a total dick! He finally came out, called formation and told us to be back by noon tomorrow. I got in the car with the girls and we left for our last night in Paso Robles.

Sunday / 4-27-2003

Both Jennie and I are sick. Christie is feeling all right, but she seems pretty tired. We just stayed in the room and ordered some barbecue. I have to be back by in camp by 1100.

At the base it was very hard saying good-bye to the girls as this is suppose to be the last time until we come back from Iraq in about a year. There were a lot of tears and hugs and sad words. This fucking sucks!

I spent the rest of the day packing for Iraq. Shit!

Monday / 4-28-2003

It was a pretty slow day today. I finished packing my bags, did my laundry, ate at the snack bar, read some magazines and a newspaper, and took a couple naps. No one knows what is going on. We're suppose to waiting for our flight and then the "box", but nothing is happening.

I called my Ma today and all she wanted to talk about was how I should move in with her and take care of her. Does she have any idea what is happening to me or is she just pretending it isn't true? My one daughter is upset about her asshole boyfriend and my other daughter was sleeping. I'm going to write letters since we're not doing anything or going anywhere now. It's weird! Nobody knows what the hell is going on.

Letter to school / 4-28-2003

Hi Everyone,

Well, we are finally in "lockdown." No one can leave the base because we are waiting for our orders to leave. We have all our gear packed in our duffle bags and are just sitting around ready to leave.

We've been told that when we get there we will be driving up to 400 mile missions. That could be from the base in Kuwait to the northern parts of Iraq. We will be bringing up some of the newly arrived tank (armored) divisions and bringing back the guys who were in the war. Also, we'll be bringing food, medicine, and water to the Iraqi people.

We have been told that the main roads are secure. Our trucks are so big that we will only travel on the main roads. We need to be careful of snipers, mines, RPGs (rocket propelled grenades), and suicide bombers. So, we will wear our flak vest and carry loaded weapons. Still, it should be pretty safe. I will take a lot of pictures and share with you.

Thanks for all your support (even though I haven't really done anything yet).

Joe (Mr. B.)

Tuesday / 4-29-2003

OK. I don't know what the fuck is going on anymore. We are back to training and everyone is acting like it's the same old shit. We went to classes in the morning and learned how to change tires on the trailer and the large tires on the cab of the truck. It was a good lesson but I thought we were leaving. It's really hot out, too.

I went to the PX for lunch and they were out of hot dogs. That's the main meal that we buy when we go there. How the hell can they be out of hot dogs? I still can't go to that fucking chow hall for lunch or dinner. We must have the worst cooks in the entire Army because the food is terrible. I couldn't even finish my breakfast today. It's the same shit every fucking day. Cold scrambled eggs, shitty potatoes, limpy, fat bacon, and some other saucy shit that I don't even know what the fuck it is. If it wasn't for the Coke machine I'd probably start shooting people. I didn't go to the chow hall for dinner today either. It was "pizza ops" night.

There is more talk of leaving soon, but it's just talk. We sure don't act like we're going anywhere. Some people are saying that we will be sent home soon and others are telling us that our DCUs (desert camouflage uniforms) will be here tomorrow. So, let's make up our fucking minds here. Are we going or not?

Wednesday / 4-30-2003

Still no word on when we are shipping out. We went on a convoy today. I'm pretty sure that they don't know what to do with us anymore because all we did was drive a long way into the woods and then have a "team ops" day. In other words, we had a barbecue, played volley ball (I didn't because of my knee), and drink beer. It was a nice day but it was a wasted day. My only real complaint was that they cooked chicken and some other shitty meat. Why can't I ever get a fucking hamburger at these barbecues?

We got back at 1630 and drank some more beer with the guys. I went to sleep at 2100 and than spent the rest of the night getting up to piss because of all the beer drinking. I'm still feeling sick from a cold or some shit.

We're wasting time and waiting for something to happen. What the hell is in store for us?

Thursday / 5-1-2003

I'm still fucking here! We're suppose to get our DCUs tomorrow. I got some extra gear today. Then I went on a compass course with a couple of my squad members. We did OK, or at least we didn't get lost. Someone saw a three foot gopher snake and went all bat-shit. All I did was stay clear of it and took the long way around.

We got back to the barracks at 1430. I've been writing letters for two hours now. Everyone is drinking again and getting ripped.

May 5th is suppose to be the date we move out. Whatever! We'll see.

Friday / 5-2-2003

It's raining today. We took a HET out and just drove around the woods with it. I'm still feeling sick so I just laid in the bench behind the drivers and co-drivers seats and tried to sleep. That was a fucking mistake as the guy driving the HET was going really fast and going through every puddle he could fine, which were all over the place because of the rain. The HET is covered in mud. He was going through mud puddles and the mud was just flying up into the air about twenty feet and covering everything. Of course, I'm thinking the whole time that he's going to lose control and we're going to turn the whole truck over one of these hills and we're all going to die. I always think the worst.

We made it back and had to take the HET to the wash rack. The driver knew of a place where there was a tube that allowed a shitload of water to come out of it. I have no idea what it was really for, but we ran the HET under it and washed the mud off.

I got back and laid around doing nothing but feeling sick. Our DCUs are in and we'll be given them tomorrow. It's really quiet in the barracks because all the drunks are still out drinking.

Jennie is coming to sneak in a visit tomorrow. It will be good to see her again. Christie isn't coming and I'm not sure why. Maybe she's getting tired of saying good-bye to me and doesn't want to deal with it anymore.

Saturday / 5-3-2003

We got our DCUs this morning. Of course they didn't have the boonie hats that went with them. Most of the DCUs we have are used. One of the guys actually got a pair of pants with a hole in them and a red circle drawn around it. That means that some active Army puke turned these pants in to get new ones and that's what they are giving us. What a bunch of bullshit! The two uniforms I got are both winter style. They have summer material that is lighter and allows more air to flow through the uniform, but I get two winter uniforms. I'm so happy because I'll be over there in the summer with a uniform that will keep me hot. Fucking National Guard!

We went on a convoy to Hunter Leggett, ate lunch there, and drove back. They have no idea what to do with us at this point. They are just keeping us busy doing bullshit all day.

Jennie came and we went to Paso Robles and got a room for the night. Most of the motels rooms were taken up with other soldiers and their families so I had to buy an expensive room. It has a Jacuzzi tub in it and my daughter is thrilled.

The club at Camp Roberts burned down tonight. It was called the 50-50 Club and it had a lot of history to it. During World War II there were a lot of movie stars who came to the club to entertain the troops. There is a small museum on base where they have a bunch of pictures of the movie stars in the club and other WWII memorabilia. I don't know what the fuck I'm going to do for lunch and dinner now. Where will I get my pizza and beer?

Sunday / 5-4-2003

They made us show up for a formation at 0730. Again, it's just to dick with us. As soon as it was over we were dismissed. Jennie and I headed back to town. We went to the show, ate a steak, and then I had to come back to camp. Again, it was hard to say good bye to Jennie, but since we've said good bye for the last time about five times, we didn't cry too much this time. Sad, but as she drove me into the camp the club was still smoking and it has burned completely to the ground. There is nothing for me to do so I just spent the rest of the day in the barracks.

Monday / 5-5-2003

We got up at 0530 today. The morning was spent packing our gear to be ready for the move. Again! I put a few things away but my duffle bags are already packed from before. I racked out the rest of the morning. I'm sicker than I've been all week.

I walked to the PX for lunch.

At 1300 we went on a convoy. Again, they don't have anything for us to do so they just let us going driving out into the woods. We stopped twice and just sat around. No practice battles, or OPFOR, just sitting. We spent the rest of the afternoon driving through the boonies.

I am really sick. I came back to the barracks, took three aspirins, ate, then felt a little better. I spent the rest of the evening writing letters and watching a DVD.

We're suppose to be real close to leaving, but I don't know. They have been telling us that for a while now. I don't know how to feel anymore. It seems unreal, yet I'm here. The big question of the day is are we going to "Demob" (go home), or "Mobilize" (go to Iraq)?

Thursday / 5-6-2003

I went to breakfast today and hit the fucking jackpot. We got eggs to order (made any way we wanted) for the first time since I've been here at Camp Roberts. Then, after breakfast, I went into town on the back of a deuce (what we call the 2 ½ ton truck that is in common use in the Army). I spent almost three hours at the local store and bought a bunch of junk for Iraq. There sure are a lot of pretty women around here. I sure could use one.

After I came back from town I just sat around outside our barracks and watched the guys play volley ball in a new sand pit the guys had built between our barracks and another building. Now, I know they don't have anything for us to do as all the platoons are decorating the outside of the barracks buildings. Ours built a volley ball court and it is the hit of the company. I didn't play as I don't want to fuck up my knee anymore than it already is.

This morning as a group of us were walking we passed our Lieutenant and saluted him. That means he had to return the salute so that pissed him off. He's kind of a regular guy and that's why he hasn't been promoted for a long time, so it was funny that he gets pissed off when he has to salute us. Usually you have to say some greeting when you salute an officer such as, "Good morning, Sir" or "Good Afternoon, Sir" or whatever. So, his greeting was, "God damn it!" We all laughed at that one.

Wednesday / 5-7-2003

I got to drive a Bradley Fighting Vehicle today. We all took a drive over to what is called Mates. It's a part of the camp where there are some full-timers working there on Army stuff, but I have no fucking idea what "Mates" stands for but, I'm sure it has something to do with maintenance. Anyway, it was really fun to drive that thing around even if it was only in a circle.

First, you get in the drivers seat and some guy explains about the gas pedal and the steering. It's remarkably simple and like driving a car. I guess that makes sense to make these things as easy to drive as possible because after talking to some of the complete idiots in the Army, some things have to be simple. After the instructions, you get to drive away. It was funny to see the different personalities driving this thing. A few of the guys would just barrel around as fast as they could and make really sharp turns and churn up the ground. The problem with trying to make a sharp turn is that is slows down the Bradley, but as it rips the ground up, it's worth the loss of speed. Of course, being the pussy that I am, I drove it a little slower than most. Then when my ride was almost over I decided to grow some balls and crank it up a little. It was fun and then it was over. That was one of the highlights of this entire activation for me. I had never driven a tracked vehicle before and now I can say I have.

We also practiced how to "battle drop" a truck off the back of the HET. We are learning this in case we are in Iraq and need to get the truck off our trailer quickly before we get blown to fuck. All you do is unhook the truck as quick as possible, start it up, and have some one roll the truck backwards down off the trailer and ramp. It sounds easy but when you are the driver, it's scary. When it came for my turn, I was nervous as hell. Of course, I smiled and acted all macho and shit, but inside I was really scared. The others made it look so easy that I knew I'd fuck it up. So, I started backing the deuce up and just let it roll. I was crooked as hell and the truck was bouncing like crazy. I made it and just sat there while all the guys were laughing their asses off at me. When I knew I was safe and the truck wasn't sticking out of my ass, I laughed, too.

The next thing we did was to just drive the HET around in the dirt with an Abrams tank on the back. Now this is one heavy fucking load. The tank weighs about seventy tons and with the weight of our HET, this was one big ass load. Nothing exciting to tell about this exercise as it was just driving around in the dusty grounds for a while.

As we convoyed back to the company area we were lucky enough to have portable shitter attached to the back of our truck. I was so proud to be driving back to our area with a shitter behind me. It was so fucking embarrassing!

We've got this one guy in our platoon that we call the Buffalo Soldier. He's a real pain in the ass and everyone wants to knock him on his ass. He's suppose to leave for Ft. Lewis today for some strange reason. No one knows why but we're all glad he's leaving. Everyone is getting fucking weird!

Letter to school / 5-7-2003

Hey Everyone,
I don't know what to write. I'm still in California. It's been getting to the point where I am embarrassed. I've been telling you that I'm going to Iraq for three months now and I'm still here.
We have all of our equipment, we have our desert uniforms, we're packed, our trucks are in Kuwait, but we're still here with no sure date to leave.
The guys are falling apart, too. One got arrested last night (reasons left unsaid), guys are getting into fights, and the bickering is constant. We are frustrated and ready to either go somewhere and do something or send us home!

I feel guilty because you've all been so supportive and kind and I haven't really done anything. So, I guess I just want to thank all of you for your thoughts and kindness. You've been important to me even though I haven't gone overseas.

Thanks,

Joe

Say "Hi" to my class.

Thursday / 5-8-2003

Today is fucked! They took us into town and gave us a free movie with a bag of popcorn. Can we just go to war already? They did it for our morale. I guess they can see that we have no morale right now and starting to fall apart, but bussing us into town to watch a movie isn't going to change anything. How about busing us to a whore house? That'd help my morale.

We came back and did absolutely nothing. I am getting depressed with this bullshit. I want this to end. I was so fucking bored that I walked to some dumbass museum here at the camp. I guess I shouldn't call it stupid as it had a lot of old pictures of all the movie stars that had been here. There were some really famous people that came out here to entertain the troops during WWII.

I went to the PX twice and spent some money on useless shit. I'm just bored beyond belief and don't know what to do for the time to pass. I want this to end. I just want to go home. Quite wasting my fucking life here.

Friday / 5-9-2003

We had sent our DCUs out to get our name tags, U. S. Army tags, and unit tags sewed on. Wherever the fuck they took the uniforms to be sewed they put the unit patches on the wrong fucking sleeve. So, everyone had to rip that off right away. Oh, and the fucking patches are green and black which is the wrong color for our desert sand uniforms. I can't believe how the fucking National Guard treats it's soldiers. We get the shittiest stuff and the Guard doesn't give a shit about us. It's a fucking joke!

We drove over to Hunter Leggett again to waste the day. We parked at some lake and had another hot dog barbecue. At least it wasn't fucking chicken or some fucking taco shit. We talked and laughed all day and no one killed anyone. So, it ended up being a good day.

Everyone is talking about demobing. I don't know how I'm going to handle it because my mind is set to not go to Iraq anymore. They have been dicking with us so long that I just want to go home and forget all about the past three months. I may go into town and pretend that I have some laundry to do. I don't really, but getting a ride into town, even on the back of a fucking Army truck, will be something to do. I just want to get off this fucking base and go into town. We're starting to joke that we are the Camp Roberts permanent party (permanent party is the troops that are assigned to a base as a full time duty station).

Saturday / 5-10-2003

In the morning I went to the PX. In the afternoon the guys finished spreading the sand on the volley ball court and I watched.

My daughter Jennie came and when we were released in the afternoon and we went into town and got a motel room. I am really happy that she drove all the way up here to spend another week end with me. It's about a four hour drive from my house, so I know it's not fun for her. She goes to college full time and works part time to help pay her school bills, so taking time out every week end to come see her Dad is pretty special. Christie didn't come again. I don't think she can take the good byes anymore.

There is no news about our deployment. We didn't even have a 1800 formation as we usually do.

Sunday / 5-11-2003

I had to come back to camp for a 0730 formation. Just another way to dick with us and make sure no one has gone AWOL (absent without leave). We stood in the ranks for a couple minutes and then were dismissed. What a waste of gas and time.

Jennie and I went back to town and went to another show. Afterwards, we bought some barbecued ribs (my favorite meal), and some chocolate for desert, and went back to the room for the rest of the day.

Jennie drove me back to camp and left at 1700. The good bye wasn't anything special because we've been through it so many times all ready. I hope it wasn't the last time I'll see her because I'd like to give her a bigger hug if it is.

We had a formation at 1900 and it was back to the barracks.

Monday / 5-12-2003

We got orders today for overseas. We have 2-7 days left here. We are going to the sandbox assigned by the 5th Army Group (some headquarters group somewhere that is in charge of a lot of shit in the Army). It hit me like a ton of bricks! I didn't think we were going anymore. In fact, our First Sergeant had the people who thought we weren't going overseas hold up their hands in our formation today and I was one of many that put their hands in the air. Then he told us about our orders. What a fucking blow!

I went to a phone and called home. I got to talk with Christie and she cried the whole time we were talking. I was close myself, but tried not to. Jennie wasn't home. I talked with my Ma and she seemed OK with it. I'm not sure if she really understands that her son is going to war halfway around the world, but that's what is happening.

All the guys are getting drunk tonight. I had one drink and drank to the lost brothers of the past in other wars and this one. It was sort of a "salute" to all the service people that have died in war. We promised to watch each other's backs and all that macho shit. I can't believe it, but we're going.

Tuesday / 5-13-2003

The plan for today is to play volleyball and then softball. While we wait to leave we are pretty much on our own to fill the day. Since I don't want to play the sports because of my knee I headed over to the internet café. It's a place set up where we can go on line for free and get some emailing in. It's an old barracks building that has been sectioned off in rooms. It's very old and dirty, but at least it has workable computers. After you sign in you either have to sit in the hall way or sit in the waiting room, depending on how many guys are there. Usually, it's not too long of a wait.

I went back to the barracks and it's a good thing I did. We are being told to pack our duffle bags for the last time because they are going to be loaded up tonight. We are suppose to have an "A" bag and "B" bag. They have given us a list of what should be in each bag. I'm not sure what the difference is because the bags are going on the same planes as we are and going to the same place. We have to stencil the bottom of the duffle bags in paint with our names, social security number, and unit. It's a bright blue with yellow letters. Very tacky!

After getting my bags packed and marked I did my laundry in a 2-gallon bag. I put an article of clothes in the bag, add some soap, and then the water, and zip it up and shake. It's not the best way to wash my clothes but it's cheap and quick.

I called my daughters and told them that I'll be leaving in the next couple days. They took it well. Like I've written before, I've said good bye so many times already that I think they are getting immune to the emotions of farewells over and over. I was proud of them nonetheless. I called my Ma and she was fine with it, too. At least we know the truth now and that is something that we didn't know for sure before. Now we're being told we could be gone for up to nine months. We'll see.

I'm getting a little nervous about this but my 2nd squad is the best, so that will help. I guess I have new brothers now.

Wednesday / 5-14-2003

I got my DCUs back today. There was no name tag sewed on, no rank, no nothing. It came back with all my patches still in the pocket and nothing on it. What a fucking joke! The National Guard sucks! One of the sergeants in our platoon went out and bought a portable sewing machine and is sewing everyone's patches on that he can get to. He did mine. It looks like shit, all crooked and messed up, but at least my shirt has the patches on it. Again, they are all dark green and black, the patches made for the BDUs (Battle Dress Uniform, which is the forest pattern), so the whole stupid idea of the patches makes no sense at all. I'm embarrassed to be wearing the uniform while it looks so fucked up and wrong. Fucking National Guard!

I laid around the rest of the day doing nothing. I walked to the PX three times because I didn't know what else to do. Even a lazy bastard like me gets bored after a while. One time me and a couple buddies even helped the lady in the PX put shit on the shelves. It's like we're stock boys or something.

Everyone is still joking that we're not really going over to Iraq. It's all a big fucking joke. I didn't even try to call my daughters today. I figured it was all said yesterday and it's not fair to keep going through the same shit day after day. I'm just waiting and waiting.

Thursday / 5-15-2003

Today's the day! We got up at 0330. The first thing we had to do was clean the barracks and get all our gear outside by 0500. It was all assholes and elbows. Our first formation was at 0600. There was the CSM (Command Sergeant Major) of California blabbing on about our duty and country and shit. Meanwhile, I'm fucking freezing standing in the dark and cold of this morning. I had a small American flag sticking out of the band around my helmet and the CSM came to me and made me take it out. What a fucking jerk-off. Didn't he just get done talking about America and being proud and shit?

O-dark thirty, ready to leave for Iraq.

After standing in the dark and cold and the wind we were loaded onto buses to go to Travis AFB (Air Force Base). It's about a three hour bus ride from Camp Roberts. Soldiers were taking a shitload of pictures on the bus. There's a lot of loud talking and fooling around. I guess it's false bravado time.

When we got to the air base we were put into a large building. We were told that we could not go outside except for the smokers, of course. So, I pretended to be a smoker and went outside just to get some air and see what was happening on the tarmac. I had put my American flag back into my helmet band and as I stood outside I watched all the TV cameras and reporters that were there taking film or pictures of me. I have no fucking idea if I was on any TV reports or made any papers with that flag in my helmet, but I thought it was cool anyway. After standing outside and breathing all that smoke I went back inside to breathe some clean air. Fucking smokers!

They gave us a pretty good lunch in the building. Nothing fancy, but very tasty. Some of the families were in the building with us. It was about seven hours from my house so I didn't even bother calling my girls. It was weird to be sitting there with all our battle-rattle on and our weapons and then have wives, mothers, fathers, brothers, sisters, and kids all around us.

We had a mass formation on the tarmac and then they marched us toward the plane. This was pretty surreal. As we're walking in one long line toward the plane the families are about one hundred feet away behind a yellow rope. They are all yelling and waving and crying. One little boy runs along the rope and yells, "Daddy, Daddy, I love you!" I can hardly keep from crying myself because of that little boy's pain. I think of my girls and I can hardly keep it together.

I get on the plane and am told to keep walking past the first class seats and take a seat in the back. I get a row to myself and lay my battle-rattle and weapon on the seats next to me. After the plane takes off I find out that the electricity is out in my section of the plane so I can't listen to music or hear the sound of the movie they are playing. Fucking perfect! I'm in the ghetto part of the plane and it's going to be a fucked up day.

We fly to Minneapolis, MN. It takes about three hours. Once there we are allowed to get off the plane for a while. We are packed into a small area of the terminal and just waiting for the next, longer leg of our journey to Kuwait. The smokers jam on a little porch and I go outside to get some air. That was a big mistake! Standing in the middle of about ten guys who are puffing away like they will never have another cigarette in a ten foot square area was hell. I lasted about thirty seconds out there before I had to come back in. Fucking smokers!

The next part of our flight took about seven hours. We flew to Amsterdam. When we were allowed off the plane we were taken into a section of the airport that we had to ourselves. While I was walking around our section of the airport I noticed a yellow rope separating us from the civilians. As they would walk by they would look at us and of course, we, starving for anything not military, would look at them. There were two young ladies that were waving at us so I walked over to them. I had someone take a picture of me with my arms around the two girls, who happened to be sisters. I told them I wanted the picture because one of the women had a sweatshirt on with the name Amsterdam on it when really I just wanted a picture of me with two good looking women. I also had a picture taken of me with one of the cops that was patrolling our area. Right after that someone came up and told us all to go around the corner and get away from the rope. Gee, I hope it wasn't something I did. Our layover was two hours.

Now, we're on to Kuwait. My legs are swelling up and I still can't listen to the movies that are playing on the plane. I don't even have a light that I can turn on to read by. What a fucking lousy trip this is turning out to be. I spent some of my time by walking around the plane to see what I was missing. I should of stayed in my seat. At the front of the plane were the assholes that ended up sitting in first class. Of course, it was our officers and high ranking sergeants. They were sitting there with their legs up and food all around them. What a rip off! Then I went up the stairs (this was a big fucking plane) to where the cockpit was. The door was wide open and I was allowed to watch them. I guess when about three hundred soldiers with M-16s and automatic weapons get on a plane the pilot isn't too worried about someone getting into the cockpit of the plane. While I was sitting there one of the crew even explained their radar scope and some of their instruments to me. The view was pretty incredible, too. There was a bench behind the cockpit and I laid down and tried to elevate my feet to help with the swelling. I felt too embarrassed to stay there long, so I got up and went back to my seat. I spent the next few hours sleeping, eating, pissing, shitting, and sleeping some more. We arrived in Kuwait City at 2305 Kuwait time. We are told to remain seated as we will be on the plane for a few more hours. Shit! My legs are starting to swell up like balloons. I have to loosen my boot laces because my boots are getting too tight. Get me off of this plane!

Saturday / 5-17-2003

Well, where do I start? We landed in Kuwait at 2305 last night. 0015 we boarded some buses that took us to Camp Wolf. It was a short drive. As we got off the buses there was a person standing there with some hand held device that recorded who we were somehow. We had to show our ID cards before we could go into this big tent that was set up for us.

They took us into this large tent and we sat on some wooden bleachers and waited. A female soldier came into the tent and welcomed us to Kuwait. She explained that we were in a waiting area and will assigned our final destination in a day or two. She told some information about what we could expect while we were staying at Camp Wolf. I don't remember any of the talk as I was in shock that I was actually in Kuwait and headed for the war in Iraq.

After our talk in the tent we were herded to another large tent that was in the middle of a bunch of similar tents. As I'm walking to this tent I'm fucking hot. It's 0100 and it's hot as shit. It's also very hazy outside. They have lights all over the place, so there seems to be a smoky haze everywhere. After spending some time in Kuwait and Iraq I discovered that the haze was simply dust from the fine powered sand everywhere in this part of the world. The tents were air conditioned and had plywood floors. Our company was put into a couple tents with nothing in them. We put our gear and weapons down wherever we could and went outside to look around.

All I could see were tents everywhere. There were some open spaces where there were civilian looking trucks parked and a lot of buses. There were also pallets full of cases of water with Arabic writing on the side. A couple soldiers were sitting on top of a pile of water and I asked if I could have one. They told me the water was for everyone and that I could help myself. I took a bottle and drank from it and spit it out immediately. It was fucking hot. I would learn in the next few weeks that the water we had was always fucking hot because it sat outside in the sun all day. Things weren't going well and I've only been here about an hour. As I walked back to the tent I was already covered in dust which was everywhere.

Back in the tent most of the guys were just standing around or laying with their head on their gear. At least it was cooler in the tent with the air conditioning on. I laid down and tried to rest.

Instead of being at Camp Wolf for a day or two we were told to get up and get our gear and get our asses outside. We were leaving already. We had our flak vest on with our battle-rattle and weapons. A bunch of smaller buses, that seated about fifteen soldiers, pull up for us to load onto. I got on the bus and took a seat near the rear door. Our bus was loaded and we sat there for awhile until all the buses were loaded with our entire company of over three hundred soldiers. There were curtains on the windows and they were shut. We were headed to our new camp in the middle of the night with curtains drawn shut. This was a little spooky and I was feeling nervous. They are being careful about us but we don't have any ammunition for our weapons yet. What the hell? During the seventy-five mile drive to our new camp I sat in the dark and peeked out of the bottom of the rear door to try and see something. As we drove down the road all I could see was sand and it reminded me of the snow along roads back in Michigan when I lived there. I started to think I was looking at snow and yet my mind was telling me that snow wasn't possible where I was right now. I'm going crazy already!

We drove off of the paved road and entered a bumpy, sandy road that led to the entrance of my new home. Ah, Camp Victory, Kuwait. What a fucking dump! It's in the sand with no roads or pavement anywhere. There are just a bunch of tents set up in the middle of the desert. I still couldn't see anything except what went by the bottom of the rear door of the bus, but when we stopped and got out, I wished I still had a curtain around my head. It was light outside now and I remember looking around and wondering if I had landed on the moon. A real fucking hellhole! We stood around and just stared. No one knew what to do next. There were a row of port-a-johns that we quickly used. I would learn to love yet hate these port-a-johns after awhile which I will explain later.

My first moments at Camp Victory, Kuwait.

We piled into another tent and put our gear down. Again, this tent was empty except for the plywood floors. Only these tents did not have air conditioning and they were fucking hot and airless. Little did I know that this would be my home for most of the next five months and we would not have any air conditioning during the entire summer months. As I looked around outside the tent all I could see was sand, dust, tents, and guard towers. And it was getting fucking hot.

After our gear showed up and was dumped into a huge pile between a couple tents we took our duffle bags into our new home and found a spot. I grabbed a spot by a flap in the middle of the tent thinking I might be able to get some air if I slept there. As the hour got later in the day I got hotter and hotter. I couldn't even breathe right. I was sweating all the time and didn't have any energy to do anything. I tried drinking a lot of water but like I wrote before all the water was hot from sitting out in the sun every day. I was fucking miserable and I've been here a whole twelve hours. After a while we were told to go get a cot to sleep on. That will be my new bed for the remainder of the time I was in Kuwait and Iraq. Great!

I went to lunch at the camp's one mess hall. It's another big-ass tent with a shitload of tables and chairs. The place is packed with people from other units and our own. There must be a few thousand soldiers on this base. As I am sitting there drinking a cold drink and trying to eat something despite the fact I have no appetite due to the heat, then the inside of the tent starts to turn red. I am not sure what the hell is happening until someone that has been there a while tells me that it's a dust storm. I had never seen anything like it before. The air in the tent became red and trying to breathe became a battle. When I walked outside to go back to my area I couldn't see fifteen feet in front of me. The wind was blowing sand sideways and it the sun was gone. An hour later it was over. This is one weird fucking place!

The HETs are here and parked behind our tents. They don't look the same any more. When we got them back in Camp Roberts, California, they were brand new. Their forest green camouflage was nice and clean. Now, they are covered in a fine sand coating and look more brown than green and black. I wonder it that's what I'll look like after being in this fucking desert for a while? We walked out to check on our trucks and it's hotter than shit. I hate this fucking hellhole!

Sunday / 5-18-2003

Another fucking hot day. We got up early, I don't even know what time it was, but I couldn't sleep anyway. We were told to go work on our trucks in the morning. I walked behind our tents the distance to the trucks and I felt like I was a hundred years old. I can barely function in the this sand and heat. We worked on the trucks until 1100. When I write that I "worked" I really just made it out to the truck and sat my ass down in the shade of the truck and sat there cursing. There is no way that I can do anything in this fucking heat. At 1100 we were allowed to go back to the tent. It's close to 120 degrees now and I have never felt a heat like this.

At lunch we walked the half mile to the mess tent and got some food. I have no appetite at all. In fact, the thought of food makes me gag. The only thing I can get down is dry cereal and something cold to drink. I'm trying to drink just water as they are telling us to drink tons of it every day and stay away from the sodas. Supposedly, sodas will dehydrate us. Too bad I hate drinking water. Our plan was to just sit in the mess tent as long as possible but the mess sergeant was screaming for us to get out asses out as soon as we were done eating because there were a lot of other soldiers who needed to eat. Since I didn't want to keep another soldier from eating I left the cool, air conditioned tent and went back into the hell of the heat and sand.

Back at the tent I just sat there on my cot. It was too fucking hot to do anything. No one was doing any work. We were just trying to survive.

We have a truck pull up to the rear of our tent with some bags of ice. We unload the ice and put it in a big green cooler that is in the middle of the tent. The guys put a bunch of water bottles in the cooler and then pour the ice on top of it. The ice melts and the water in the bottles is still warm and crappy tasting. Nice waste of ice.

I feel asleep about 2130 and slept pretty good. I only got up once to take a piss. The weird part was that I actually got cool enough to put a sheet over me. I finally get some sleep.

Letter to school / 5-18-2003

Hey Everybody,

I am in Kuwait about 50 miles from the border of Iraq. It is so hot here I can't believe anyone wants this place. It was 120 degrees yesterday.

I got in Kuwait Friday and when we got off the plane at midnight it was 90 degrees. It's hazy and hot. I have a wet rag on my head at all times, even under my boonie hat or helmet.

There is water everywhere but drinking it is like drinking warm bath water because it sits outside all day. We are told to drink at least one quart per hour.

The sand is a fine powder and gets in everything. I woke up this morning with my eyes crusted shut because of the sand.

Walking to chow is an adventure in itself. As you walk very slowly (no one does anything fast here), you sweat like crazy. When I get to chow I don't even want to eat because I'm so hot, but if I don't I know I'll get sick. So, I sit, eat, and sweat into my food. Then I walk back to the tent during the day that because it's so hot, no one stays in. We sit in concrete bunkers. We are out of the sun and sometimes get a warm breeze. That's where I'm writing this letter.

I never knew a place could be so hot and miserable. I hate it here.

We will be doing missions soon into Iraq. There are still snipers around. We've been told that kids will run in front of our trucks so we stop, then they fire on us. We'll see.

I sure wish I was back in beautiful Ventura instead of this hellhole.

Joe (Mr. B.)

Surviving in the Bunkers

During the first few days in Kuwait we just sat around and sweated. When we landed in Kuwait in May the daily temperatures were over 120 degrees. Coming from the cool climate of California's Camp Roberts, where the temperature had been in the 40s at night and the 70s during the day, 120 degrees plus we were not ready for. It was hard just to breathe much less to do anything that took physical activity. The tents were a trap of the heat, but afforded shade. It was a messed up situation, to stay in the tent out of the blistering sun and roast from the elevated temperature, or go outside to catch the 120 degree breeze and bake in the sun. There was one place that attracted soldiers like flies to shit. The cement bunkers. These were rectangle blocks of cement, like an inverted U, with a flat top. There were two gun ports staggered on each side. In these cement bunkers was the closest think to relief we had. You were protected from the sun, yet the hot breeze could flow through the structure. One of the negatives was that there were a lot of stones these bunkers were placed on. It was hard to sit or be comfortable because every couple of seconds your ass would hurt from the stones. One soldier brought his sleeping mat out to sit on and the rest of us caught on fast, although the stones worked holes into the mats quickly from the pressure of our asses. If you could find room to lie down in the bunker, you could try to sleep a little. Most people just laid there and sweated. The less you moved meant the less energy you had to spend. People sat against the side walls of the bunker with their feet up on the opposite side, or legs folded up in front of them.

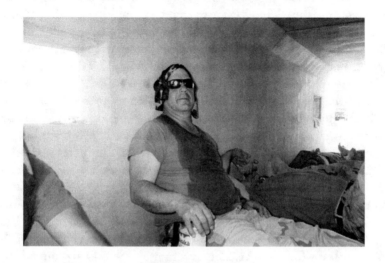

I'm trying to cool off in a bunker.

No one usually spoke during the first few days because we were so drained of energy. A bottle of water was next to everyone. Some drank it, some dumped in on their heads, and some just let it lie there. This would go on all day. One person would leave and another would take his place. After a few days the bunker became a sort of meeting place. The group you hung out with would gather in the same bunker and talk, write letters, or just try and sleep. Most soldiers resented the ones who came out early and laid down taking up a big chunk of the bunker. It didn't seem fair that they got all that shade and others had to find another place to try and stay out of the sun and heat. Normally, no one would say anything although once in a while someone would just cuss them out and sit really close anyway. That usually got the message across. Some people would just push themselves into the bunker and make room for themselves. Although we didn't appreciate these people, we understood why they did what they did. Anything to escape the heat made sense over there. What didn't make sense was what the hell we were doing trying to live, work, and fight in this heat. One soldier, who had been stationed in the Middle East during the Gulf War, brought a small kiddie pool with him. He blew it up and placed it into the bunker, which fit perfectly against the sides, and walked back and forth from the water point with filled washing tubs of water to fill it. It took several trips and a lot of sweat in the heat to fill the pool up. The water from the water point was always hot because it just sat in an iron tank in the sun and heated up all day. So, no one got into the pool right away and you had to earn your way into the pool by helping fill it. After a day of the water sitting in the pool it would cool down to a temperature that you wouldn't think was possible. It was heaven in the desert. We would sit two at a time facing each other side by side. The others waiting would sit close by and wait patiently for their turn. When I was waiting for my turn I would secretly wish everyone in the pool would just get the hell out now. I wouldn't say anything lest I make the pool gods angry and lose the chance to get in. I can remember sitting in the pool feeling completely comfortable and seeing someone walk by or drive by sweating like crazy. They would look in the bunker and see me sitting in the pool with a smile on my face. The person would stop, take a double take, and usually laugh and make some kind of comment like they can't believe the things they see over there. It was one of the few times I've had a smile on my face in the Iraq War. That pool saved my sanity on more than one occasion. Some people would sleep on top of the bunkers during the night. There was one soldier who slept in the bunker during the day in full uniform on his sleeping mat and would stay up all night. I could never figure out why he did what he did, but he did this every day we were at Camp Victory in Kuwait. During the first few days in Kuwait, and the unbelievable temperatures of 120 degrees to 130 degrees, the bunkers saved us.

I'm standing next to a bunker outside of our 3rd Platoon tent.

Monday / 5-19-2003

It's hot as fucking hell today! I guess this is the payback to the cool night last night. It's the hottest day so far. We worked on our trucks until 1100 and then quit for the day because of the heat. I love the fact that we quit working at 1100 but even the morning heat is unbearable for me. I just sit in the shade of the trucks as much as possible and drink as much water as I can get down my throat.

After 1100 I just sit in the bunker. I didn't even go to lunch today because I don't have an appetite anyway. Besides, I'm gagging all the time now either when I'm by the stink of the port-a-johns or with the smell of food. I know I'm going to have to eat sometime, but right now I can't keep anything down.

My friend bought a phone from a local Hagi (this is the name we called any foreigner in either Kuwait or Iraq) so we can call home. Great! I can't wait to use it and call the girls.

A guy who was here in the Gulf War brought a kiddie pool with him. He filled it up and I had a chance to sit in it. It felt great! The water was cool and after sitting in it I felt human again.

I slept pretty good this night but I've had a headache all day.

Letter home / 5-19-2003

Hi Girls,

I hate this fucking shit hole! It's 120 degrees again. The past two days I've spent 4-5 hours sitting in the cement bunkers with just my shorts on. I take my sleeping pad (because of all the rocks) and try to stay cool. If you call staying cool with a 120 degree breeze blowing through. I am so fucking miserable I can't believe how utterly shitty this place is.

Yesterday I experienced my first sandstorm. I was sitting in the chow hall and all of a sudden it turned red outside. Completely red! Then a cloud of fine dust-like sand blew in the tent. It was hard to see even inside the tent. Then we had to walk back into it. The sand got into my eyes, mouth, everywhere. After about one hour it quit. What a shitty place!

We're getting our trucks ready for missions. We're suppose to start soon.

Jennie, send me the sleeping mattress (or Christie), more powered drink, lip balm, and anything that will help me stay cool.

I haven't taken the handkerchief off my head in three days. I just keep it wet and hanging over my head. Everyone is miserable.

It gets light here about 3 AM and by 4:30 AM almost everyone is up. That's the only time we can do things without sweating like pigs. I clean my area and today I did my laundry. I clean my clothes in a tub and hang them outside the tent. They dry in about 10-20 minutes.

I can't wait until the mission is done and I can come back home. I miss you terrible and all the comforts of a real life. I never dreamed it could be this bad.

I love you both,

Dad

Jennie—
I love you a bushel and a peck,
a bushel and a peck,
and a hug around the neck.

(this was a song I used to sing
to Jennie when she was a child,
so, I wrote it to her in my
letters home).

Christie—
xxxxxxxxxxxxxxxxxxx
ooooooooooooooooo

(sixteen was Christie's lucky
number, so I always wrote the
sixteen hugs and kisses signs
for her)

Thursday / 5-22-2003

I went to sick call today. I've been sick for over four weeks and now that I'm in the desert, I've had headaches, dizziness, and have felt really weak. I sat outside in the sun waiting to get into sick call and just sitting in the sun and heat was enough to make me feel weaker. After I got inside the tent I sat on a stretcher that was up on a stand. A medic took my vitals and my blood pressure is still too high. Again, I don't know how they expect my blood pressure to be low after not eating, being sick all the time, and being halfway around the world about to drive into harm's way. But, their answer to my problems is to "drink more water." That's what they tell everyone here who isn't feeling well. "You're not drinking enough water." If I hear that one more time I'm going to shoot somebody and it won't be an Iraqi. I can't drink any more water than I already do.

I came back and just went into the kiddie pool. I stayed there for about three hours and felt better. In fact, I felt great!

The latest rumor here is that we will go back home by July 15th. Even though that's a lot quicker than we thought, it's not soon enough. I want to go home now!

I took a walk around the camp with a friend in the evening. I took some pictures of some of the things here. There are a shitload of trucks, cranes, tents, and soldiers. It's a pretty busy camp. When I came back to the tent everyone was just sitting around doing their thing. We're all just winding down after another day in the desert with really nothing to do.

Letter home / 5-22-2003

Hi Girls,

It sure was hard when I called you, Jennie. When you started crying I just lost it. After the call I had to stand outside by myself to compose myself.

Sorry I missed you, Christie. I would have loved to talk with you, too. I will try to call about once a week. I don't know if I can, but I'll try.

Couple of good rumors. I've been hearing a lot lately that we will be sent home by the 15th of July. This is a strong rumor, but again, nothing is for sure. The second rumor is that we might get air-conditioning for our tents. If that is true, life will get much better than it is.

I made friends with a guy that has a pool. He put it in the bunker and the water stays cold. I sat in it today for about 3 hours and I feel so much better.

When I called you, Jennie, it was 6 AM here on Thursday, and 8 PM for you on Wednesday. Weird, huh? We are ten hours ahead of you.

I love you guys and miss you a bunch. I hope I see you in just a couple months.

Love,
Dad

Friday / 5-23-2003

We got up at 0430 today. Fuck! We had to go to our trucks and pretend to work on them until 1100. They allow us to quit at 1100 because by then the temperature is well over 120 degrees and no one can do anything anyway. I feel sick all day. I have a headache and feel spaced out except when I'm in the kiddie pool. My blood pressure is down and lower than it's been in years. Damn it! I was hoping that my blood pressure would zip up and they would get me the fuck out of here. Today was another unbelievably hot fucking day. I spent most of the day in the pool. I had to help fill it up and that is a pain in the ass itself. Walking back and forth from the water point with a tub full of water in the heat is almost too much for me. But, I keep thinking of the reward of sitting in the cool water and keep moving.

Laying in the pool next to our tent in Kuwait

I spent part of the night talking with my teacher friend. I slept pretty good until I had to get up to piss at 0300.

Saturday / 5-24-2003

I can't believe it! We had a camp wide police call (what the Army calls it when you walk in a line and pick up all the trash you see, including cigarette butts). They lined up everyone in the camp at one end and had us walk through the entire camp picking up trash. There are about 10,000 of us here, or so I'm told, and it was a shitload of people. I could barely walk the distance through the camp and I sure as shit didn't pick anything up. I especially don't pick up cigarette butts because I don't smoke and I'll be damned if I'm going to pick those dirty fucking butts off the ground for some lazy ass smoker. Fuck 'em!

Our tent got a big cooler for everyone to use. It's a big green box where we can store stuff to keep cold.

Some Haggis came to clean out the porta-a-johns. It stinks like nothing I've ever smelled before when they clean those things out. You have to realize that these port-a-johns have a lot of shit in them from all the people that use them and they sit out and bake in the sun hour after hour. Everyone moves away from the area when the cleaning gets done.

I spent some time just sitting under the cammo netting that has been put up at the front of our tent. I'm trying to get out of the heat of the tent and still stay out of the sun with the netting about. It didn't work out too well. It's just too fucking hot here for humans.

I'm trying to stay cool outside the 3rd platoon tent in Kuwait.

I felt bad all day. I took a malaria pill today and have the shits ever since. What a fucking lovely war so far.

Letter home / 5-24-2003

Hi Girls,

I got my first malaria pill today and it gave me the shits. God damned Army. What a shit hole! It's day 8 and I'm still fucking miserable.

We got a huge cooler for the tent today. After putting 48 bottles of water in it, then pouring over 5 bags of ice over it, all we got was melted ice water with warm water bottles. God, I hate this fucking place.

I take my water bottle, cut the top off, fill it with ice, and then make a powdered drink. I am all out of my stash so I've been mooching off the other guys.

I also have a spray bottle that everyone uses. It dries off me so fast it's nuts!

I did my laundry this morning. I use 2 big plastic tubs, one to wash in and one to rinse in. All by hand. I hang my stuff outside and it's dry in ½ hour. I hate this fucking place.

Doing laundry.

It's been close to 130 degrees the past two days and summer isn't even here yet. I sure hope the July 15ᵗʰ rumor is true. I want to come home so much I could almost scream.

I enclosed a money bill from Iraq. When you guys are done showing it or looking at it, put it in my top drawer of my dresser for a souvenir.

I love you both and can't wait to be with you again. Notice the new address on the envelope.

Love,
Dad

Sunday / 5-25-2003

I actually got cold last night. That was weird.

We have our first mission for tomorrow. We are suppose to take some engineering vehicles up to Baghdad. So, today we had to change our helmet covers from the forest green camouflage to the desert camouflage. We also got live ammunition to load in our magazines and weapons. We each got 120 rounds. Some of the ammo are tracers as we are suppose to load up every fifth round with a tracer. We spent the day packing our gear, cleaning our weapons, loading our magazines, and buying snacks for the road. I'm nervous but ready to go.

We had a dust storm today that almost blew the tent over. There are three large poles that hold up the middle of the tent and we were fighting like crazy to keep them standing upright. The whole platoon was working together to keep the tent from blowing down. The sides of the tent were flapping in the wind and we were trying to throw sandbags on the bottoms of the flaps to keep them closed. The fucking sand was everywhere.

Letter home / 5-25-2003

Hi Girls,

Well, today we were assigned our first mission. Tomorrow we drive to Baghdad. I don't know what we'll be picking up there, but it will be about a 4 day trip.

I bought a bunch of snacks for the trip and packed my bags. We will load our ammo later and I have to clean my M-16. It's so hard to keep anything clean here but I'm not leaving this base without cleaning it.

Cleaning my weapon prior to a mission.

I am looking forward to going simply because it's cooler up there. Also, I'll finally get out of this shit hole and see some of the country. I'll take a lot of pictures.

Try not to worry about me. I know once in a while you hear about something bad happening over here, but there are about 250,000 of us and that's a lot of safe people. The guys I'll be going with are good guys and we'll take care of each other. I love you both a great deal. I miss you terribly. I'll write again when I can.

Love,
Dad

Monday / 5-26-2003

It's day #10 here and nothing's changed. It's hotter than fuck! I go lay in the pool as much as I can and as long as I can. I carry around a squirt bottle filled with water that I spray myself with all the time to try and keep somewhat cool. I soak a bandana in water and wrap it around my head and it helps a little. The problem with the bandana is that it is so stained with sweat and dirt that it stinks like my ass. I am constantly searching for ice to put into my powered drinks or water. I'm miserable all the time and feel like shit. We are still waiting to find out if we're going to Baghdad or not. I need to go. I need to get the fuck out of this hell hole of a camp.

The eight day mission to Baghdad was cancelled. I guess some unit had taken up the equipment last week. Does anyone know what the fuck they are doing here?

At least the dinner was good today because of Memorial Day. Nobody gives a shit that it's a holiday but we are happy that we get extra special food. They had lobster, steak, and a lot of other shit for us to eat. There were a couple cakes that had some pictures done with frosting that must have taken someone a shitload of time to do. They even had the mess hall decorated with a bunch of red, white, and blue shit. Very festive. Too bad it's in the fucking desert halfway around the world from home.

I called Ma today. It was good to talk to her. I miss everyone.

Tuesday / 5-27-2003

We've got a mission today. We are headed into Iraq for about eight days. We loaded up our trucks in the middle of the day and heat. And then, they cancelled

---

it again. Fuck! We had to unload the trucks and go back to the tents. All done during the middle of the day when the temperature is around 130 degrees. What the fuck!

I'm sweating my ass off while just laying in the tent on my cot. Even when I don't move I'm still sweating like crazy. It's the same shit every day now. It's so hard for me to get through these days. I gag all day long, I have no energy, and it's hard for me to do anything. And, I'm fucking hot all the time. I hate it here and want it to end now!

Wednesday / 5-28-2003

We finally got a real mission today. We went to Camp Virginia, which is still in Kuwait. We actually went. We left about 1630 and arrived at Camp Virginia at 1830. I slept on a cot on the back of the trailer of my truck. Kuwait is a vast wasteland. There is trash blown by the wind everywhere. It's dusty power-like sand and there is nothing to see. Even though it was good to get the fuck out of Camp Victory there is really no joy in going to another shitty place like Camp Virginia. We're headed for Baghdad tomorrow. It should be a 8-10 hour trip. We have to wear our flak vest, helmet, and take our M-16s which will be loaded with live ammo. Every fifth round is a tracer in our mags that we'll be taking. This is for real!

Thursday / 5-29-2003

We were up at 0430. We loaded our trucks and are ready to go to Baghdad. My battle-buddy and I named out truck "Jenny C" after our two daughters named "Jennie" and "Jenny" and the "C" was for my daughter, Christie. We drove for four hours. What a fucking waste land it is here. We sat at the border of Kuwait and Iraq for a couple hours waiting to cross into Iraq. It's fucking hot! After crossing the border we drove through a couple little towns. There were kids all along the road begging for food and water. It was very sad. The little girls tug at my heart. We spent the night in a real sandy fucking camp called Camp Cedar I. One of our trucks got stuck up to it's hubs.

When I wrote letters home to my daughters during my missions into Iraq I kept a running journal style letter going for the entire mission. The following letter is one of those.

Letter home / Thursday / 5-29-2003

Hi Girls,

I'm at the border of Iraq waiting to get fueled up for the second part of today's trip. As soon as we leave this place we load our weapons. It's kind of scary.

It's hotter than fuck and we have to wear our flak vest and helmets.

There is absolutely nothing to see here. It's desert, flat and boring. Imagine Lancaster (a desert town in California that we all lived in for two years) ten times worse.

It will be my turn to drive next. I will be driving over the Iraq border. Whee!

We're in Iraq. We crossed the border about 4 PM. The first thing we saw just broke my heart. There were little kids, some as young as 2-3 years old, lining the road, waving and giving us the thumbs up, and begging for food and water. It was so sad I almost started crying, and I was driving. The ones that got me the most were the little girls. They would have on long, flowering, colorful dresses. They would run along side our trucks and wave and beg. It was very stressful for me.

Then I got to drive through a couple of towns. What a trip! There are no rules and people drive all over the place. It's a good thing that we're so big because they don't mess with our trucks.

Back to the kids. Some would run out to the road and wave, some would give us the thumbs up or down, some gave us the finger, and some threw rocks, and last but not least, one little boy waved his penis at us. Blown up buildings every once in awhile as well as blown up tanks or trucks.

This place is so sad. I hope we can help these people but right now it just looks like they are suffering.

We got done driving at 1 AM last night. I slept on the trailer on a pad. Sand, dust, heat. I'm miserable!

My battle-buddy says "Hi."

Friday / 5-30-2003

It's 8 AM and we just got done staging our vehicles (parking them in a line). Immediately Iraqis came to our trucks trying to sell Saddam money, bayonets, flags, coins, even hash (dope). One car stopped and the guys held up whiskey bottles. They swarmed us for about 30 minutes until the MPs (military police) drove up and told them to "get the fuck out of here" and "move your ass." Very strange situation.

A Hagi trying to sell me a bayonet and money in Iraq.

I want to give them water and food but then I won't have enough for myself. I ate a MRE (meal ready to eat) for breakfast and I'm drinking warm water. I haven't showered since we left Camp Victory. Ugh!

Wearing this flak vest all day in the heat is unbearable. We have to have our helmets on, too, plus our M-16s are loaded. Scary, yet fun. I miss you two so much. I never realized what good kids I have. I love you both!

I gotten eaten up by mosquitoes last night. It's a good thing we are taking malaria pills, I guess. I get sick every day from them but what the hell. I still can't figure out how the mosquitoes breed because I haven't seen any water here. Strange land.

The base camp we stayed at last night was nothing but a dust bowl. The shitter was like in the movies of Vietnam with the half can under the hole. Thank God I didn't have to go.

Cedar I

On the first mission we pulled into Camp Cedar, which was a refueling point in southern Iraq. We lined up on the highway outside of the refueling point. It was a base set in the middle of nowhere and as every place else in this war, sand, sand, and more sand. The sand was very fine and powdery, and it was deep. We pulled off the road into the trails that lead to the fuel points. There were trails of tires everywhere so no one was certain of the correct way in. You just followed the truck ahead of you and hoped they knew where they were going. Of course, the truck in front of us didn't and got stuck in the sand. The sand was so deep and powdery that the truck sunk into it like it was quicksand. The wheels just spun and shot up sand high into the air. Every time the driver spun the wheels in reverse then forward the truck just dug a deeper hole. We put our truck in all-wheel drive and low gear. There is a control panel inside the truck that actually allows the driver to let some air out of the tires and fill them back up without leaving the truck cab. When in the loose sand, using all these things made the difference between being stuck and not. We pulled around the stuck truck and proceeded to the fueling point. The driving was very slow and it seemed as though the truck would get stuck at any moment, but we finally pulled up to the fuel. Looking behind the point you could see the tents and living quarters of the soldiers that were stationed there at Camp Cedar I. This was one of the times that I actually felt sorry for someone else besides me while I was in Iraq. Their tents were coated with the powdery sand and there were wooden toilets that had the Vietnam style half can under a wooden hole that you did your business in. At certain times they would have to burn the waste by adding fuel into the drum and lighting it up. The black smoke would float lazily into the air and permeate the area with the awful stink. They had their water stacked up on pallets in the sun like we had back at Camp Victory in Kuwait. This was right after the war in May of 2003, before the refrigerators and freezers arrived. Their clothes were hung on the ropes that pulled the tents taunt, and as they dried in the sun they also collected a lot of sand from the trucks going in and out of the camp. The constant driving of trucks throughout the camp made it a virtual dust bowl with no clean air at any time. Our convoy spent the night there because it was almost dark and to be on the roads after dark was asking for an attack. We circled around and parked along a berm of sand near the entrance. This being our first mission, we were not savvy to the ways of sleeping on the road yet, so I set up my cot alongside of the truck. As dark arrived I laid down in my cot and tried to sleep. First, it was hot, and there was no breeze here. I just couldn't stop sweating, and that made it hard to relax and sleep. Then trucks were passing within feet of our trucks and coating my sweaty body with the powdery sand. We had no cold drinks as we hadn't gotten a cooler yet and didn't know about buying ice from the Haggis. Then there were the mosquitoes. I couldn't figure out where they were coming from because I hadn't seen any water yet in Iraq. Didn't they need water to breed? They started biting around dusk. I had sand flea bites all over my feet and ankles, mosquito bites all over my body as I laid and tried to sleep in just a pair of shorts. I was sweating like I had just run a marathon, and I was as thirsty as it's possible to be. Every few minutes another truck would pass by and cover me in even more sand. In other words, I was miserable to the bone. I laid like this for a couple hours and couldn't get to sleep although I was exhausted. I got up and sat in the cab of the truck for a while, but the mosquitoes were biting so much I couldn't get any relief from them. Sleep was impossible. At about two or three in the morning I got up and put two folding chairs up facing each other. I sat in one and put my legs on the other and threw the mosquito net over my body and head. I dozed on and off until I woke up in the early light and a group of soldiers were doing police call (picking up trash, called "policing' the area) around our truck and me. I threw the mosquito net off my head and sat thee wondering what kind of hell was I in.

I'm sitting in two camping chairs with mosquito netting over me next to my truck, just waking up at Camp Cedar I in Iraq.

The mosquito net helps but it also cuts down on the amount of air you get. It's a tossup whether you want all the air you can get because you're so hot or whether you don't want to be bothered by the mosquitoes. There were some nights I went for the air when the mosquitoes weren't so bad and other nights the net just had to go up. Later on I learned how to string the net up over my cot. I got up, drank some warm water, splashed a bottle over my head, and loaded up for another day on the road to Baghdad. Camp Cedar I was the worst place I saw during my tour of duty in Iraq. The people that had to live and work there are true hard-asses because they had nothing but sand and heat as their companion. One night was enough for me.

Saturday / 6-1-2003

Good morning from Baghdad International Airport. We drove until 11 PM and got here in a slight rain. I can't believe it! It rained! Actually, the closer we got to Baghdad the better it got. Nothing great, but after looking at nothing but brown sand for over two weeks it was a nice change. I slept on my cot alongside the truck. It rained on me twice. The second time it was 5 AM so I just got up.

Yesterday, while I was driving, I killed a dog. There was nothing I could do about it. He just ran out in front of me. I felt bad about that.

We went through some towns yesterday. The streets were lined with crowds of people selling all kinds of junk, yelling at us, and staring. All the kids giving us the thumbs up. Some women slightly smiling from their black robe outfits. Very sad situation here. I wish I could give these people food and water because that's what most of them yell.

There is constant sand blowing. We had to drive through a sand storm for about an hour last night. We had the windows rolled up because of the blowing sand which made us sweat like crazy because there was no air. It was hard to steer the big truck through the crowds of people because they get so close. There are no rules for the drivers, they just go where they want to. But, they get out of the way of us because we're so big. I'm always nervous I'm going to hit one of the kids but I keep going.

There are Army trucks all over the roads all the time. There is a lot of shit being moved over here.

I'll keep this letter going during our trip to Baghdad, sort of a journal. You'll have to share it with Grandma (my Ma) because I can't write this over again.

There are a couple of things I've promised myself because of the time I have spent here. One is, I will never sit on the beach in the sand again. Maybe a rock or something will be OK, but not in the sand. I will never drink plain water again. I'm sick of it already. I'm not going to allow myself to be hot again if I can help it. So, the heat is off all the time when I come back. And, I will never take you two for granted again, as well as my house and good things in it. I hate this hellhole!

We just unloaded our cargo on the airport base. Pretty impressive! We had about 23 of the big trucks unloading grading bulldozers, etc. We did it pretty fast.

I took my first shit in Iraq today. Sat over a big, deep hole with just some wood sides. I talked with the guys on either side of me like it was nothing. It was the first time we've been able to shit in three days. Unbelievable conditions here.

Oh yeah, our convoy got shot at last night. I heard the two "pops" and didn't think too much of it (I did pick up my weapon, though). Nothing was hit. Lousy shot.

We're trying to get today's mission on the road but as usual, everything is all fucked up. It's after noon and we're still not on the road and we're not suppose to drive after dark. Yet, both previous nights we've been on the road until almost midnight. This unit is so fucked up.

Sunday / 6-2-2003

I finally got some sleep last night. We're at another base somewhere around Baghdad. It's called Camp Dogwood. There is just sand and Army people. We put our cots on the trailers and slept there. It was nice and cool and I just passed out until 5 AM when we got up. It's a new day. We'll see what happens. Oh yeah, there were wild dogs running around all night barking. I saw a lot of blown up tanks yesterday.

A blown-up Iraqi tank along the road to Baghdad.

We drove through one place where there must have been a hell of a fight. Our convoy got lost a couple times yesterday. Once we stopped right in front of a Republican Guard barracks. It was blown to fuck. We were watching the flank (side) of our trucks and I was walking up and down the line telling the guys to be alert. It was kind of scary. There had been a hell of a fight there and I had a bad feeling. First time in my life I ever felt like that.

My Best Drink Ever

Camp Dogwood, just south of Baghdad. We're picking up some equipment to bring back to Kuwait. Everyone has something to pick up. Most of the vehicles that our convoy is picking up are drivable, and some aren't. Some have to be hoisted up with a crane, some pushed with a tracked vehicle, and some wrenched on. My battle-buddy and I had to wench ours on. We were one of the last to load and it was around noon. It's over 120 degrees and we start to work. I remember walking back and forth between people trying

to get the correct info about the vehicle we were putting on the back of our truck. Active Army guys are happy to be getting rid of their broken down junk and their area cleaned up. My driver and I work, sweat, and work some more. It took a couple tries to line up the HET trailer to the broken down track. After a couple hours of hard, sweaty, miserable work in intense heat and sun, the truck is loaded. We line up the HET and wait for the others to drive back to our staging area for the night. A soldier comes up to our HET and has a bag of cold sodas. He offers up a strawberry soda. I taste is and I am in Paradise. Nothing has ever tasted so cold and so good! I drink what I think is half and hand the can to my battle-buddy. I craved that taste again. After that mission I always had the same brand of strawberry soda with me, but it never tasted as good as that one at Camp Dogwood after a hot afternoon in the sun of Iraq. To this day I keep the same brand soda in my refrigerator at home. Every time I drink one it reminds me of the best drink I've ever tasted.

It's 2:30 PM and we have worked all morning loading broken down vehicles on our trucks. I can barely function in this heat. I don't know how these people keep going in this heat. I feel so weak all the time. I thought I was getting stronger because I had been feeling better, but I was wrong. I am losing weight, though.

When I get home I want to get a couple gallons of good ice cream. I want some cherry soda, cheese sauce and chips, and all the stuff I like to eat. We get nothing cold here and nothing good. I haven't even had a shower in four days. One week end a month, my ass!

I'm gonna end this letter and start another one to you. Please share this (read to) Grandma because I could never get all this written again.

I love both of you very much and am looking forward to being home with you soon.

Love,
Dad

Monday / 6-2-2003

Today we drove back toward Kuwait and Camp Virginia. It was a long, boring, fucking hot ride. A part of the road was totally fucked up. The pavement ended and there was just sand for almost 90 miles. As we drove along this part of the road our trucks were kicking up huge clouds of dust. It was so dusty that there were times I couldn't see the truck that was ten feet in front of me. There were convoys passing us going back north and that contributed to the clouds of dusty sand, too. It's bumpy as hell and our gear is flying all over the place. As we got closer to Kuwait the heat goes up. I fucking hate Kuwait.

Once in Camp Virginia we combat dropped our loads. It's hot as hell. We actually got lost on the base itself today. Everything is fucked up here all the time. We have terrible leaders. Our transportation company is the worst ever. We were not suppose to drive through towns because they told us it was too dangerous yet we drove through a shit load of towns going and coming. Stupid fucking Army!

Letter to school / 6-3-2003

Hey Everyone,

I know by the time you get this school will be out for summer break, but I thought you'd like to hear about the children here.

I'm in Iraq. I've been on the road for a full week, wearing the same clothes, no showers, no cooked food, no cool drinks. We drove up to Baghdad and now we're on our way back to Kuwait.

I have seen thousands of children, young as 2-3, lining the roads, begging for food and water. It breaks my heart to see them. We are told not to throw them food because they may run in front of the trucks to get it, but we do anyway.

Kids begging for food and water along the road in Iraq.

This country is a mess. Our convoy has been shot at twice, with no one hit. I've seen many blown up tanks, trucks, and buildings. There were a couple of places close to Baghdad where you could tell there was some fierce fighting by all the blown up stuff.

I sleep outside every night on a cot with the sand blowing constantly.

This place is terrible. I miss my home and family terribly and if I think too hard about the way things are right now, it drives me a little crazy. I can't wait to be back in Ventura.

Joe

Letter home / 6-3-2003

Hi Kids,

I'm still on my way back to Kuwait. We're somewhere in southern Iraq headed toward Basra. Today there was an explosion about 200 yards to the front of our convoy. I thought be were being attacked with mortars (little bombs shot by a tube). Then another one blew closer to the convoy. I started yelling, "Let's get the fuck out of here! Let's go!" Turns out it was some Army guys in Hummers blowing some explosives they had found. My battle-buddy started laughing at me because he could see the Hummers and I couldn't. He's such a jerk! There is a mean streak to his sense of humor and I am starting to not like him very much.

Mortars Along the Road

Driving on my first mission our convoy came to a stop along a stretch of the supply route named MSR (main supply route) Tampa heading up to the Baghdad Airport. I was the third truck from the front of the convoy. As we sat on the road we were still new to the war and didn't get out to pull security as we were expecting to move right away. As I was talking with my battle-buddy an explosion happened about 100 yards from the front of the convoy off to the left. I high cloud of dirt rose into the air about 100 feet high. I immediately knew it was the explosion of a mortar round. I excitedly stated that we were being attacked and if we didn't get moving, the rounds would find their mark. I couldn't understand why we were still standing still. Then another round went off even closer, then another almost immediately after the second one. I was really excited now and scared that the insurgents were finding the range and walking the mortar rounds into our trucks. I started yelling out the window, "Let's get the fuck out of here. We're being mortared! Why aren't we moving?" I'm sure no one could hear me above

---

the loud running of the engines of several HETs and the commotion of the mortar rounds going off. I just couldn't understand why we weren't moving out of range, or at least trying. After a few moments of shear terror on my part, and my yelling out of the window, my battle-buddy started laughing. He told me that he could see that some MPs were up ahead and had stopped the convoy in order to set off some mortar rounds that were planted along the roadside (IEDs or improvised explosive devices). I stared at him in disbelief until I could see that there were no more blasts and no more danger. As the convoy started up and passed the MPs, I couldn't stop being angry at the suddenness of sheer terror on my part without knowing what was really happening. Why didn't people tell us what the hell was going on before they started blowing things up? This would be the first of many times, that because of a lack of communication, I would think we were under attack and be scared for my life. The next time we stopped my battle-buddy couldn't stop laughing and telling the story over and over to whomever would listen. It took weeks for me to live this story down. But, thinking of my initial reaction to the explosions and sitting still in a very large truck (the nickname we had for our trucks was "BFT" for "Big Fucking Targets"), thinking that I might be blown to hell any second still makes me think of how scared I was at the sheer terror of war. The chance your life could be taken away from you in such a random manner made being in Iraq a constant challenge to keep your sanity. How could real life be so crazy?

Continuation of letter home / 6-3-2003

We passed another group of soldiers who had stopped a car and truck along the road. They had about six guys lying on the ground, tied up, and they were guarding them. I drove within ten feet of them. I remember thinking, as I looked down out of my drivers side window, that there are still a lot of bad people around and this is for real.

I got done driving after six hours. It was the hottest and most boring ride I've ever been on. Nothing to see except sand. A part of the road is all sand so I had to slow down until the dust cleared so I could see. It's awful!

Well, I found out that what blew up were a couple of mortar rounds. Only they were set off by our own MPs. This place is so crazy! I still can't believe I'm here and it's been over two weeks. God! Get me home!

We stayed at a refueling point which is just a place in the sand where we can get gas. There are no bathrooms, showers, or anything else. But they did have an excess amount of fucking mosquitoes. I got bit so many times I even have bites on top of my head. Finally, about 2 AM I got some bug juice (insect repellant) from someone and fell asleep sitting up in the cab of my truck. Turns out no one got any sleep last night because of the mosquitoes. They got us up at 4 AM and it is now 7 AM. We haven't moved. Our leaders are so fucked up. We get lost every day. We sit around and waste daylight every day. And we just have to endure stupid stuff every day. It's incredible how little they really need us here. I have no idea why we came, but shit, we're here.

I am so smelly. I have been in the same uniform for one full week now. Ugh!

We're suppose to drive through Basra today. That's where some of the roughest fighting was during the war. Should be interesting.

We're back in Camp Victory in Kuwait. It's hotter than hell and the wind is blowing like crazy. It's a minor sandstorm right now. I hope it doesn't get worse.

Three weeks today we've been here. There is still no fucking mail. This place sucks the big one.

It's getting too windy to write so I'll wrap this one up.

It turns out we weren't even suppose to drive through any towns because it's too dangerous. Way to go leaders.

I sure hope the rumor of coming home around July 12th or the 17th is true. I've already had enough.

I love you both very much and miss you so much it hurts.

Love,
Dad

Wednesday / 6-4-2003

We're back at our base camp, Camp Victory, in Kuwait. I'm fucking miserable. It's the same shit. I can't eat, I'm gagging all the time, and there is still no fucking ice here. AHHHH!

Thursday / 6-5-2003

I've been here for three weeks. It seems like forever. It's hot as usual. I repacked my ruck sack so the next trip up north I will be better prepared. I cleaned my M-16 today. Yesterday I ate a burger that a buddy bought for me at the local burger stand (some private companies have set up some small trailers here at Camp Victory that sell things like burgers, pizza, and ice cream). After eating that burger I ended up having to get up at 0330 with cramps. I ended up shitting my brains out in the port-a-john in the middle of the night. Damn! I'm so sick of this place that I can hardly remain sane. I hate it!

Friday / 6-6-2003

I QUIT!

This was the last entry into my daily journal. From this point on I only have letters and stories that I had written during my time in Kuwait and Iraq.

Letter home / Friday / 6-6-2003

Hi Girls,

Well, we're back on the road again. We spent the night at a base nearby. We loaded up some engineering equipment, bulldozers, etc. We're taking them to the Baghdad Airport. It'll be about a 4-5 day trip. It's 6:35 AM, we've already eaten breakfast, and we're waiting to begin the day.

It's 12:30 PM and we are packed into a refueling station at the border of Iraq and Kuwait. It is hotter than fuck! When we drive down the road the air feels like fire on my skin. We're sitting inside our large metal cans (trucks) during the hottest part of the day. They are telling us we have to stay here for four hours but we don't know why.

I broke the weld on the passenger's seat today so we can use it as a recliner. So, I took a nap while my battle-buddy drove. I woke up in a puddle of sweat. This flak vest is very hot.

I am so pissed at our leaders. We waste a lot of driving time because we park so long. It's really frustrating because it's so miserable to just sit in this heat.

I've been talking to a lot of guys I've met on the road from other units and they say they are leaving after only about four months here. So, we are all hoping July will be our month.

I'm hot, feel ill all the time, and miss you two like crazy.

Saturday / 6-7-2003

Well, were do I start? We convoyed until 1 AM. We're not suppose to drive during the night, yeah, right. We're not suppose to drive through towns, yeah, right. We drove through three towns last night. Exactly what we're not suppose to do. It's interesting to see all the people out, how they line along the road, etc., but it's dangerous, too. One guy had his hand on his dick the whole time we drove past him. The children still break my heart, so cute and little, begging for food. We throw away most of our MREs but we can't throw it to them. Doesn't make sense to me and it frustrates me.

Someone said they heard a couple shots last night. I didn't.

We're sitting by the roadway ready to roll to Baghdad. People are coming up to us trying to sell us Iraqi money, souvenirs, ice, coolers, and even whiskey. The MPs race up in a Hummer and chase them off. As soon as the MPs leave, the people come back.

Last night I slept on my mat on the back of the trailer. I draped a mosquito net over me.

Ready for sleep on the back of my trailer somewhere in Iraq.

I actually got too cold so I climbed into the cab and slept sitting up with a steering wheel in my chest. Never enough fucking rest.

It's 1:05 PM and we are in the Baghdad Airport. We just unloaded the construction equipment on our truck. We always end up working during the hottest part of the day. I am so hot and tired. It seems like I can barely hang on whenever I work. I hope this doesn't last too much longer because it's taking it's toll on me. I close my eyes and picture myself back at home in the yard, or in the living room, or mostly, in the cool water of the ocean. I need to come home.

It's now 1:50 PM and we're parked along a roadway that goes into the airport. We're trying to get to the PX here on the base. If we do I'm buying some pop (soda). I'm tired of drinking fucking water. I don't feel any better with it anyway.

There is no breeze as we're parked next to a wall. Sweat is covering my body. Everything I touch is hot.

I got a small scratch on my arm about one week ago and now it's infected. I suppose I'll have to go see the medics when I get back to Kuwait.

There is a large building across the way that is blown to shit.

It's 2:15 PM and we're just sitting in our trucks at the airport waiting to find out what's next. It's hotter than hell on the tarmac as we just sit here.

We have sat by the side of the road twice today. They tell us that the roads are unsafe yet we park and give them a big, stationary target. God! Our leaders are stupid!

I bought some ice from a local Hagi at one of the stops. We have to rinse our cans (sodas) and bottles of water off because their ice is unsafe. But, it keeps the sodas and water cold, and that's what's important. I've given up on the water shit. I drank nothing but water for almost three weeks and was miserable the whole time. So, I figure, what the hell? At least I'm enjoying myself once in a while.

I saw one of Hussein's palaces today just outside the airport here in Baghdad. I took a picture with my cheap ass disposable camera, but it was probably too far away.

We've been on the road for three days and we're not half done yet. At least time goes quicker when I'm on the road.

Everyday I touch the Wonder Woman and Sylvester dolls on the back of my helmet for luck (my daughters gave me little toys of these characters for luck).

I love you guys.

Showing Wonder Woman and Sylvester on the back of my helmet.

It's 3:20 PM. You're not going to believe this one. We left the airport (secure area), went into the city of Baghdad (not a secure area), then turned around in the city and came back to the airport. We are now sitting in our tin can trucks, sweating our asses off, going nowhere, sitting somewhere we already were. Our leaders are all assholes!

Near the airport there are trenches where the Iraqis burned oil during the war. It goes for a couple miles and burnt the area to shit.

I'm going to try and stay cool. Ha! Even my own breath is hot here.

Just a couple of thoughts about the past twenty-four hours. We got lost three times last night. Everyone is pissed at our lieutenant. One of these days he's going to get someone hurt, or killed, by being in the wrong place at the wrong time. Or, he'll get someone hurt by accident because we're driving at night. What an asshole.

This morning I had to shit under our truck because there were no bathrooms. I can't believe how I'm living. I'm never going camping again. I'm never drinking plain water again. I'm never going to sit in the sand again, and I'm never going to be hot again. No heat in the house when I get back home, girls. When I get home I want a gallon of good quality chocolate ice cream, strawberry soda, apple pie, cheeseburgers, and cheese sauce with tortilla chips.

Sunday / 6-8-2003

It's early in the morning. We're parked on a road ready to, get this, go back to the airport in Baghdad to pick some shit up. We were just there yesterday.

I bought ice from the locals last night and some soda. I bought for the guys. By the way, Jennie, I need some cash. We loaded up out coolers, set up our cots on the back of our trailers (with mosquito nets), and took a shower (remember the $5 plastic shower bag I bought)? The shower was the hit of the night with all the guys. Then I racked out about 9 PM.

We got up at 5 AM, cleaned up, and were back in the truck. Every morning I feel sick. I don't know if it's my meds, my age, or both. But, I feel shitty all the time.

It's 7 AM, Sunday here and 9 PM on Saturday where you are. Sometimes I try to picture what you're doing . . . dreams.

I've been here almost one month and I am as miserable as I was the first day. I can't believe how much I hate this hellhole.

It's 2:50 PM and we're still waiting in our trucks, and it's fucking hot! I put my bandana in my helmet and pour water on it. Then I wrap it around my head like a pharaoh. Then the extra water that I used to soak the bandana in my helmet spills over my head as I put it on. In other words, I pour water into my helmet, soak the bandana in it, let it sit for a while, and dump it on my head. My battle-buddy laughs like crazy when I do this, but it helps keep me cool and I don't care what anyone thinks here. I use a water spray bottle to spray myself all the time. It's the best thing that I bought. It's always a constant battle to stay cool.

I keep dreaming of the day I'm home running into the ocean back in California and stripping this fucking uniform off.

Monday / 6-9-2003

It's 5:45 AM. I've been up since 4:30 AM. These guys are crazy. I didn't sleep at all last night because there was no air, it was too hot, and being on the tarmac of the airport meant helicopters taking off all night. I woke up once under my mosquito net and thought I was suffocating.

I took a shower on the tarmac last night using the plastic shower bag hanging off the trailer. I had a picture taken of me and my bare ass so I could remember the event. How many people can say they were butt-ass naked on the tarmac of the Baghdad International Airport?

*I'm taking a shower on the tarmac at the
Baghdad International Airport in Iraq.*

We loaded trucks on top of our trucks until dark last night. This job is one of the hardest I've ever had. There is a lot of physical stuff.

It's 7:40 AM. We just left the airport and I came within inches of taking out a pole. I'm driving on a one lane road at a curve, and a Bradley armored vehicle is coming the other way. So, the end of my trailer is about to hit the pole as I'm facing this Bradley. I had to back up and straighten out. I held up the entire convoy.

The Back Road Into BIAP

After the first few missions to Baghdad International Airport (BIAP), renamed Bush Airport by the troops, the main road into the airport became too dangerous to travel. So, a back road into the airport was now the way our convoys entered. We turned off a highway and onto a narrow two lane paved road that went by some nice looking homes on the north side of the road and one of Saddam's mansions on the south side of the road. The mansion was on top of a hill, and I wondered why there was just one hill in the middle of nowhere until someone told me it was man-made. As we traveled toward the airport on this narrow road, we would take up our normal "more than one lane" because of the width of our trucks. If a convoy was coming the other way, we had to get as far over as we could and not try to fall off into the ditch alongside part of the road leading into the airport. Pulling a trailer that was wider than the lanes of a road was never easy, although being able to destroy anything that got in our way, such as other cars, small buildings, guard rails, poles, etc., certainly made things easier. We would drive down the road easily at the beginning of the entrance to the airport because that part was fairly straight. After a while the road would start to wind back and forth a little with poles close to the road and not much room to err. If the road was clear in the opposite direction, it wasn't too much trouble to navigate through the turns. As stated before, if there was a convoy coming the other way, that was a different story. On our way out of BIAP one day we met up with a convoy of Bradley Fighting Vehicles. These are tracked vehicles that take up any room they want and no one but a tank will argue with them, certainly not my truck, even though it was the largest truck in the Army. I was driving on the winding part of the road with a wall to the south of me and a pole approaching the north. A convoy of Bradleys were coming the other way. The first Bradley came up to the curve and stopped, waiting for me to pass. With all the skill I had in driving the HET for one week back at Camp Roberts in California and the past few days of just aiming the truck down the road in Iraq, I was about to lose this small battle of HET vs. Bradley. I passed the pole and started my turn. One of the great things about the HET system is that the trailer, having forty wheels to support the weight of a seventy ton tank on it, can turn easier than a normal semi truck because the trailer wheels can turn independently around a corner.

The HET trailer can turn in a much shorter radius than a normal truck that just swings around the corner. Even with this advantage, the last boogie wheels were not going to make it around the pole without taking it down. Here I was stuck in front of several Bradley vehicles, with trucks lined up behind me and people everywhere watching the mess. My battle-buddy had to get out and hand turn the wheels on the trailer as far as they would go as I backed up the truck. I started my approach again and cleared the pole by inches. With my battle-buddy back inside we drove up the road now with our forty trailer boogie wheels out of line, that is, crooked. The first chance we got we straightened up the wheels, but the damage to my pride was done. I had failed the "pole" test miserably and gave a show to many people who were probably telling their battle-buddies what a shitty driver I was. The one thing about that episode is that I always wondered why the Bradley stopped for me. They usually never stop for anyone other than a tank. Was he messing with me? Did he set me up for failure? It was several days before the guys let me forget this show of my driving skill, or lack of it.

Previous letter continued:

It's 10:12 AM. I just got done driving for two hours. I'm sweating like crazy, and my left arm is burnt to a crisp from the sun. It's already unbelievably hot. I hate this fucking place! There is still twelve hours of driving to go today. AHHH!

It's 2:10 PM. It has to be the hottest day yet. The air coming through the truck windows is burning my skin. I keep spraying myself with water, wetting my bandana and putting it on my head (it really stinks because it's so dirty). I found out if I put some water in my helmet and let it sit for a while, when I put it on my head, the water is cool and soaks my shirt.

The little kids come running out of their homes when they see us coming. They wave and smile hoping for food. I've been throwing the candy that I get in my MREs once in a while, but that's not too often. I always wait for the little girls to be by themselves so I know they'll get it. If there is a boy or a man with the girls, they end up taking the candy or whatever it is we throw to them. The little girls are so cute. The older ones are all dressed in black and won't even look at us. They sure fuck the women up here as they get older. These bastard men over here need their asses kicked.

I'm fucking hot!

It's 4 PM. I think a U.S. service person died today. We passed another convoy and there was an accident. As two Army trucks passed in opposite directions on the two lane highway, they clipped each other. One body was wrapped in a poncho and another was being shielded with one. So, that person must have been messed up if they didn't want anyone to see. That's a dangerous part of this job. We drive on a two lane *highway sometimes and our trucks take up more than one lane because of the trailer's width. We pass other large Army trucks all the time and we are all going as fast as we can. That's why I actually wear my seat belt when we're on a narrow road.*

It's really crazy here. I left my notebook with this letter in the sun and this paper is almost too hot to rest my hand on. Everything is hot, from all the parts of the truck, to the stuff in the truck, to everything on our bodies.

While we were driving before I was dozing off (I wasn't driving). Some kid must have been yelling as we passed him because for a split second I thought I heard one of you yell, "Dad." I ached for you both at that moment. I love you and miss you a great deal.

Tuesday / 6-10-2003

I just got up. It's 4:30 AM. I had a terrible time sleeping last night. I was hot all night as there was no air and no breeze. I took a piece of ice from my cooler and rubbed it all over my chest to cool myself down. It was 130 degrees yesterday. I can't believe it's going to get hotter because summer is coming. God help me!

I shit on Iraq! Literally! I took a shit in the dirt this morning. Unbelievable how I'm living. I hope this trip ends soon so I can clean up and wash my clothes. What a rotten way to live.

It's 11 AM. You won't believe this. We just drove about ten miles down a desert, bumpy, fucking hot road to a camp called New York in Kuwait. It's in the middle of nowhere, just like our Camp Victory. It's like some guy is pulling a cruel joke on us. The sweat is pouring off me. This paper is burning my hand. Help me!

It's 10 PM. You're not going to believe this one, either. They took us to chow for lunch around noon, in this Camp New York. Then they never came back to the chow hall to pick us up. We sat in the mess hall for 4 ½ hours in, and get this, an air conditioned tent. It was just the break I needed! I ate a meal, napped in a chair, and felt alive again for the first time since we've been here. It was great!

With that, I'll end this letter because we're headed back to base camp after six days. I love you both dearly and think of being with you constantly.

Love,
Dad

Letter home / 6-19-2003

Hi Girls,
Today's topic? People I have to live with.

1. *The guy next to me who is constantly putting cream on his hands, folding all his clothes like it matters, sits on his cot in the dark and does who knows what, freaking me out, constantly brushing the sand off his cot despite the fact we live in a windy, fucking desert, who always has to have his fucking radio on.*
2. *The big, dumb ox who butts in on everyone's conversation, even when he doesn't have a fucking clue what we're talking about, who never does a fucking thing.*
3. *The high pitched, dumbass broad with the fake boobs who thinks she is so cute, that no one can stand, except;*
4. *The guy who is having an affair with her while telling everyone he loves his wife and kids.*
5. *The idiot who is so selfish he turned his bunk sideways so he could have double the room, who uses one cot just for his shit, who has gone to Russia in the past to find a wife and was mad when she left him, who no one can understand because his English is so bad.*

Just a few of the people I want to kill!
I love you both. I miss you like crazy. I want to be home with you.

Love,
Dad

P.S. Sandstorm today . . . AHH!

The sand is always blowing in Kuwait and Iraq.
I'm on the left with a battle-buddy.

Letter to school / 6-27-2003

Hey Everybody,

Well, I don't know about you but I am not enjoying my summer vacation.

Today, I had guard duty at the main gate from 8 AM to noon. The first two hours were OK because I was in a tower with a cover surrounded by sandbags. The last two hours were not so good. I had to stand in the sun with full uniform on, flak vest, helmet, and loaded weapon. The sand was blowing so much I had sand in my weapon and everywhere else.

I have guard duty tonight from 8 PM to midnight. It should be cooler and less windy, I hope.

Guard Duty

Pulling guard duty at Camp Victory in Kuwait at the main gate was no treat. Uniform on, flak vest on, helmet on, and a couple of loaded magazines for my weapon. We gather at the MWR (moral, welfare, and recreation) tent for the ride to the gate. The LMTV (light, medium, tactical vehicle or truck) is parked outside. We slowly walk to the truck. There is never a ladder in the truck that is suppose to be there. They are designed to have the ladder stored underneath the bed of the truck, but most of the time the ladder is lying loose in the back of the truck or is missing altogether. You put your weapon on the floor of the bed of the truck, grab the side, and pull yourself up. The first step is a big one for a short-legged guy like me. Sometimes I climb up the side of the truck, from the tire to the boards on the side, and over to the seat. At least there are things to grab as I go. I move down and take a seat on the wooden bench on the inside of the outer wall. Everyone is quiet, for the most part, and everyone holds their weapon differently. I put mine barrel down with my hands resting on the butt end. Some leave theirs lying at their feet, and some across their laps. The tail gate is put up, locked shut, and the safety strap is clicked across the end. The truck takes off, and you feel every bump in the dusty, sandy road. The dust comes up and into the rear of the truck and covers everyone in the back of the truck, so you try not to be the one on the end. The truck goes slow because we're driving past tents of soldiers walking around or sitting on the cement bunkers smoking or talking or both. When you get to the gate, people climb out and almost run to the choice positions. The guard towers are the best. In the day's heat and sun, you can get a little shade, and if you have enough sandbags, you can pile them up to make a seat. There is one tower even with the gate, and it's manned by the SAW (squad automatic weapon or machine gun) operator. The other is placed far back of the gate and is basically the

—

last line of defense if someone were to attack. This one gives you a clear view of the gate and some distance to react to any problem. This is where I take my position. During the day the sand blows and I put my sunglasses on and wrap a scarf around my neck and pull it up over my nose.

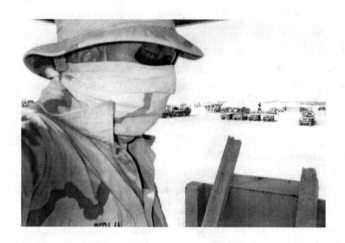

I try to keep the sand out of my eyes, nose, mouth,
and other openings in the guard tower.

Every minute or so I have to wipe my sunglasses free from the dusty sand that clings to them.

I'm standing guard in the tower at the main gate at Camp Victory, Kuwait.

I sit low on the sandbags and peer over the ridge that protects most of the rest of me but my not my head. I have a rag loosely wrapped around the bolt action part of my rifle to keep the sand out and give me a chance to fire if I need to. As I watch the people work at the gate and the people to my side work on their trucks in the motor pool, I wonder what the hell am I doing here? The fact that I'm in the middle of the desert where someone chose to put an American base in Kuwait seems so surreal. The SOG (sergeant of the guard) brings water and checks to make sure I'm awake. I can't help but be awake with my ass going numb from the sandbags I'm sitting on, the sand blowing all around and seemingly through me. I sit, think, sweat, and watch my time until I'm relieved. Another job at the front gate is the side that lets military vehicles in. This is pretty easy. You stop the lead vehicle, ask to see their trip ticket (paper work that every vehicle needs to have in the military), and find out how many vehicles and personnel are in the convoy. You remind them to clear their weapons (make sure that there are no bullets in the weapons), and send them on their way. The dust raised by the vehicles surrounds you and sticks to you everywhere and just adds more misery to an already miserable duty.

Standing guard at the front gate.

Another duty is checking vehicles that need to enter carrying goods or workers into the camp. These vehicles must be searched as well as everyone in the vehicle. A mirror is used to see under the vehicle and doors are opened as well as trunks and hoods. Each person is patted down. I have only been the one who holds my weapon at the ready while others searched the people and vehicles.

*I'm guarding the truck driver while someone else
checks the truck for explosives.*

I used to think that guard duty was a joke until I went to war. Even though we were at our "safe" base camp in Kuwait, I still watched every person all the time with my finger close to the trigger. A couple of episodes stand out during my tours of guard duty. The road that leads out of camp has no traffic that enters. One day a car came up toward the gate on the exit road. I immediately took cover behind a cement barrier and aimed my M-16 at the driver's window. Everyone else at guarding the gate took cover and pointed their weapons at the car. The car stopped short of our positions. I don't know if he saw us ready to light him up or he just stopped realizing his mistake. We signaled to him to go back and he did. He then came back up the correct road and told us he's just made a mistake. This was one of two times in Iraq that I was within seconds of shooting at someone in a car. I have often wondered if this man had any idea how close he came to being killed that night. Another incident was when a man and a woman (Americans) came walking up the road to our gate at night. We had our flood lights on, and they just walked out of the darkness. We halted them and found out their van had gotten stuck in the sand on the way in. It just seemed so bizarre to see an American man and woman walking toward out gate at Camp Victory in Kuwait. At night I used to sit in the darkness behind the area that was lit up by the flood lights. Some soldiers sat in the light and talked, but I kept thinking, what if someone wanted to kill one of us. If he can't see me, chances are he won't shoot me. So, I stayed in the shadows. There was a highway about one hundred meters from the gate and the lights of cars and trucks would go by. I just wondered where someone would be going at 2 AM in the middle of the desert in Kuwait. Fours hours on and eight hours off, and then you repeated your guard duty. The best shift was 8 AM to noon and 8 PM to midnight. You got your night's rest and stayed out of most of the heat, except for the hours of 10 AM to noon. Guard duty was always thinking time, at least during the night hours when there wasn't a lot going on. I'd think of home, the family, what I was doing halfway around the world with a loaded rifle. Even though I was surrounded by people, the loneliness made me feel like I was the only person on the planet. I hated guard duty!

Letter to school continued

Your comments about the graduation dance were great! I could just picture the eight graders going the limit on the dance floor and you walking through the middle of them. It's a great visual (the principal had written how the eight graders were "grinding" on the dance floor and how she had to break the mobs up at the dance).

Yes, soldiers are getting killed over here on the average of one every two or three days. We are all nervous when we leave this camp. They are hitting convoys and that's us. Two more died yesterday and that's not including the attacks we don't hear about because no one died. I'm scared but continue to do my job. I am so looking forward to being a teacher again.

The campus sounds great (improvements were described in a preceding letter from my principal). Any word on my assignment for next year? The latest rumor is we'll be back in the states by late August. But, other rumors have me home by Christmas, too.

As far as things I need, I could use some envelopes, pens, snacks that won't melt, lip balm, sun block, and anything to keep me cool.

I sure wish I was home in the "June Gloom" (a foggy time of year in Ventura, California).

Thanks for writing. It means a lot.

Joe

Letter to school / 7-2-2003

Hey Everyone,

I hope you had fun on the 4th of July. I'm not sure what we will get here to celebrate. Probably some special meal that taste like sand, like every meal.

This place is so strange. So different from regular life back there. Last night I was on guard duty at the main gate. Things were boring until a Hagi (Ha-gee), what we call the locals, drove up the wrong road. Immediately all seven of us took cover and brought our weapons up to the ready. I was behind a cement barrier. Turns out the guy just made a mistake. I wonder if he knows how close he came to being killed? Things are real here and it's scary.

I want to be home living a normal life again. I can't wait to be home with my children and trying to be the best damn teacher I can. I miss my life.

Joe

Letter to school / 7-5-2003

Hey Everyone,

Yesterday was the 4th of July and very depressing for me. Knowing everyone was having all that fun with family and friends while I'm stuck in this shit hole (excuse my French) was tough.

But the worst part was across the road was a company of soldiers all packed and waiting for the busses to come and pick them up for the ride to the airport and a plane ride home. When the busses showed up I wanted to run and jump on one so I could come home, too. Rough day!

It's over 120 degrees today and it's not even noon yet. I'm starting to forget why we are here. I sure don't think this place is worth one American soldier's life.

I hope you had a great 4th of July. I sure miss my life.

Joe

Letter home / 7-9-2003

Hi Girls,

My duties are getting better! Last night I was on CQ (Charge of Quarters). It's where someone has to stay up (or at least pretend to stay up) and answer any phone calls or deal with any problems at night while everyone else sleeps. Well, the tent I will be working in every other night is suppose to be air conditioned. The air conditioner was broken last night, of course, so I spent another sweaty, no sleep night. But, when it gets fixed I should get some good sleep.

Now, today I'm what they call the "Shower Nazi." I stay in the trailer that we take our showers in and make sure the water is cleaned off the floor (I use a squeegee) and make sure people don't take too long and use too much water. But the best part is the trailer is air conditioned. I sit in there from 1:45-3:15 PM and then again from 8:30-10:00 PM. So, I'm getting out of the heat for part of the day and if they get that other air conditioner fixed, I'll be getting some good sleep every other night (unless something happens, of course).

The Shower Nazi

Back in Camp Victory, Kuwait, we were able to take showers every day. We could only take one shower a day because of the Shower Nazi. We could also only take a few seconds of time under the water in the shower because of the Shower Nazi. There were two times during the day that we were able to shower. The afternoon shower time was 1330 to 1500 hours, and the evening time was 1930 to 2200 hours. There were several trailers with showers in them throughout the camp. Ours was behind our five living tents. From the outside it looked like any trailer, only without windows. There were a few steps leading up to the door in the middle of the trailer. As you entered there were eight sinks to your right. Four on one side and four on the other. Between them on the end wall there was an air conditioner that was always on full blast. To the left of the door were the shower stalls. About twelve of them with six on each side of the trailer. A curtain hung on the outside with just enough room to stand and clean on the inside. All the shower heads were removable so you could get the sand out of your ass as well as all the other places it ended up. Some people went to the sinks to brush their teeth or shave. I always went straight to the shower side. Sometimes we had to wait outside in a line with the Shower Nazi opening the door letting you know when and how many could come in. There was one bench in the middle of the shower stalls with hooks on the outside of the stalls to hang your things on. I would only go in the shower trailer with my flip-flops and shorts. Other people wore robes, shirts, shoes, and seem to bring everything and the kitchen sink in with them. I always got a bang out of the people bringing in towels. It was over 120 degrees and I would dry off in seconds after leaving the trailer without having to dry myself with a towel. You were suppose to go in the shower, turn on the water, get wet, then turn off the shower and soap up, and then turn on the water to rinse. As soon as you were done rinsing you were suppose to get out. I always followed this pattern, not because I wanted to save water, but because the water smelled so bad that I would gag almost the whole time I was in the shower. So, I wanted the water off as much as possible to keep from puking. The small piles of sand in the bottom of the shower stall never seemed to go down the drain. I would walk out into the night air, and for the one time during the day I would feel cool for a few seconds as the slight breeze blew over my wet body. There were actually times that I felt a little cold and that was a few seconds of heaven in hell. The Shower Nazi's job was to make sure no one spent too much time in the shower, no one let the water run too long, no one was taking too much time at the sink, and especially making sure no one just stood around enjoying the air-conditioning. Every once in a while the Shower Nazi would have to take a large squeegee and push the water that laid over the floor toward the drain in hopes it would go down it. During the afternoon shower time there were never too many people taking showers because there were still too many hours of sand blowing left. There was a period of time when a few people went to the afternoon shower and seemingly never came back out. Then I found out why the day I had to be the Shower Nazi. They were going in there to just sit or lie on the bench and enjoy the air conditioned air instead of being in the afternoon sun and temperatures of over 130 degrees. This lasted until the Company Commander found out and put an end to the afternoon escape plan. Walking through a narrow space with a bunch of naked men sure made me miss the privacy of my shower at home. In defense of the bad temperament of the Shower Nazi, the one night I had to pull the duty showed me just why the Shower Nazi was always pissed off. If you had to spend over two hours cleaning up after a bunch of naked guys, you'd be pissed, too.

Letter home continued

Today's topic . . . sand fleas. I have a couple hundred little bumps on my body that are barely noticeable yet itch like crazy! These are from sand fleas. They are so small you can barely see them unless you feel them biting and look closely at them. Their bodies are almost transparent and they have wings. Their bite itches for days and the bumps stay on you even longer. They itch, they itch, they itch. Seems like every morning I get up I have a bunch more.

It's another 130-140 degree day. It figures I would be here for the hottest part of the year in one of the hottest places in the world. The "Berlin Curse" strikes again.

Jennie, I hope you had a good visit back in Michigan with Grandma. I'm sure you did.

Christie, I hope you had a good time with the house to yourself and I hope the landlord doesn't want us out (that last one was half joke, only half as I hope you behaved).

Well girls, I love you both and miss you a bunch. I can't wait to get home.

Love,
Dad

Letter home / 7-13-2003

Hi Jennie and Christie,

Well, I finally got the package with the drink mix and vitamins. It was in a large orange mail sack with a note attached saying, "damaged goods." Seems one of the huge cans of powdered drink mix you mailed came open and there was powder all over everything. It was pretty funny. Since the poppers (little firework poppers) didn't get here by the 4th of July I decided I'd save them for the day we leave this shit hole.

Sandstorms every day this past week. All my stuff is covered in sand every evening. I clean it off, then the next day it starts all over again. Still fucking hot! Today is the 150th day of our activation. I think that is quite enough time spent in the Army at this time of my life.

I enclosed a picture of a freezer. I want you to buy a little one like this and put it in the corner of the living room. Use it for frozen food and, here's the real reason, I want bags of ice in it when I get home. I never want to be without ice again. I want to be able to get ice whenever I want.

OK girls, you need to talk to each other about sleeping arrangements when I get home. I want you to have it settled and my room ready for me as soon as I am back. You fix it yourselves. I don't want to come home and have to figure it out. I just want to relax! Be fair and be nice about it.

Jennie, don't worry about writing all the fun stuff you're doing back home (she felt guilty writing about having fun when I was in Iraq). I want to hear about you having fun otherwise being here means nothing. Freedom!

Your hotel adventure sounds nuts, and a lot of fun. First item for the house is dishes. Christie, I'm glad you had fun on the 4th of July. I wish I could have been there, too.

I'm glad you guys finally got the right address for me. I've been writing it for a month but no one looked at it. Tell Grandma, too.

Girls, I know you are both doing things the way I hoped for. Be polite, be civil, and work together. I miss you a bunch and love you even more. I hope to see you in August.

Love,
Dad

Postcard home / 7-14-2003

Hi Girls,

How hot is it here? Well, today a professional football team's cheerleaders were here for the troops and your dad didn't go see these hotties because I didn't want to walk a quarter mile in the fucking heat! It's up to 140 degrees today and I am fucking miserable! No date for the homecoming yet. I hate not knowing. I miss you both and love you both like crazy. I am so ready to come HOME!

Love,
Dad

Sitting and sweating in the tent, as usual.

Postcard to school / 7-14-2003

Hi Everyone,

How hot is it today? It is so hot that a professional football team's cheerleaders are here and I didn't go to see them because I didn't want to walk the quarter mile in this unbelievable heat. It's 140 degrees today! No word on a homecoming date yet. All kinds of rumors from August to December. Heeeeeelp!

Joe

The Walk to Chow

Every day, while in base Camp Victory in Kuwait, started with the walk to the chow hall (a big tent) about a half mile away. I would put my PT uniform (Army shorts and t-shirt for physical training) on for the walk. Most guys would be in uniform, but I was already too hot for clothes as the temperature was close to one hundred degrees at 0600 hours. The DFAC (dining facility) would only let you in with your uniform or your PT uniform. Stupid rules ruled Iraq and Kuwait. First, we would leave the front of the tent and the little shade offered by the cammo netting overhead. Across the gravel and over the powdery sand road into and through another area of tents. Cutting through the tents there was an open area with a square berm (pile of sand) area for waste water. We would then follow the road toward the DFAC.

The gang walking to chow.

Near the end we passed a set of port-a-johns and any port-a-john always smelled the same, TERRIBLE! The odor of a lot of people's shit and piss in a small container that bakes in the sun in over 120 degree heat made me gag every time. Cutting through another row of tents, a motor pool (where they parked and worked on trucks), and another open area, we arrived at the DFAC. There was a water buffalo (a metal tank filled with water) outside to wash your hands. Some people did, some did not. If it was really hot, I didn't waste the energy to walk twenty steps out of my way. A short row of plywood led to the entrance, and a sergeant always stood by the door to make sure you were in uniform and looked clean (the DFAC Nazi). Stupid Army rules! The first month I had no appetite and could barely get any food down. I ate dry cereal and toast and drank water. Everything there made me gag. I never went to lunch because by then it would be so hot that I couldn't walk to the DFAC without getting sick. One day at Camp Victory there were some professional cheerleaders that came to entertain the troops. I never went because I knew the walk to see them would make me sick. The walk for dinner was hard because it wasn't much cooler than it was at noon, but by then I needed to eat something. I've never walked as slow as I did in Kuwait and Iraq. I was always tired, always had a headache, always in powdery sand, and always, ALWAYS TOO FUCKING HOT! I would watch others walking, talking, laughing, and wonder how they did it. And then I'd remember that I was fifty-three years old and they weren't.

Letter home / 7-16-2003

Hi Girls,

Well, by the time you get this I will have gone and come back from a mission in northern Iraq by the Syrian border. Yes, I'm back doing missions again. I felt it best to be with my buddies and take the same risks they do. It's all about loyalty to battle-buddies. I'm sure it's hard for you to understand why I would put myself in harm's way for inner pride, but I had to for peace of mind. I'm sure I will be safe and it'll just be more stories to tell.

Wednesday I'm sitting in the truck ready to get it fueled up. My truck is going to another camp in Kuwait called Camp Doha. We're suppose to pick up a forklift to take up north. I will be back in our base for tonight and will leave tomorrow morning for Iraq. It is hot and I've forgotten how sweaty I get in my uniform when I'm working in the sun. Once I'm driving I'm OK, it's the sun and the physical work that kicks my ass. I think of you both constantly and hope that I get to come home to you very soon.

Thursday It's 7 AM. I've been up since 4 AM. Our trucks are loaded. I'm sitting in the truck waiting to leave for the day. I will be in southern Iraq later today. Everyone is nervous because of all the attacks on convoys lately. To be honest, I am a little scared going into northwestern Iraq near the Syrian border. That is a very unfriendly place, but I feel confident and the odds are on my side. I love you both.

10:30 AM We are at the DMZ (demilitarized zone) between Kuwait and Iraq. We just had a briefing telling us what's been happening in Iraq and it's all bad! I will wear my helmet and vest the whole time. It's really hot already, just like every day. We'll only be driving for another four hours, then we will stay the night in a camp called Cedar. It's a safe zone. I love you both!

Writing a letter while on a mission in Iraq.

4 PM We made it to Camp Cedar. It's fucking hot! It has to be 130-140 degrees. The sun is shinning right through the front windshield while we wait for fuel. The ride was terrible! It was hot, boring, and hot. Did I tell you it's fucking hot? So far the trip has been totally safe. I hate this fucking place!

Friday It's 7 AM Iraqi time. I slept in a dust bowl but it did cool off real nice last night. I even pulled the cover of my sleeping bag over my body. Too bad for me another convoy moved out at 2 AM and woke me up. My back is getting sore from sleeping on a cot for the past two months. I sure wish you would have sent the self-inflating mat I bought for this. I left the box next to the desk. You must have put it away when you cleaned and forgot about it. Save it for when you have a guest over instead of them sleeping on the floor.

Well, we're headed into a dangerous part of the journey. I wonder what today will bring.

It sure was a pretty night last night with the stars out, sleeping on the back of the trailer. It would be a million times better if it were a Ventura night. I love you both!

4 PM I'm at the Baghdad Airport. What a fucking trip! It started OK. We drove for a while then we hit a part of the road that is bumpy and dusty for about ninety miles. The dust gets so bad that you can barely see the front of your hood. At one time there were four HETs side by side dusting each other trying to get to the front out of the dust. It was very unsafe and stupid on the driver's part (I was not driving). We stopped during that stretch of road and got out for a break. All of a sudden, there was gunfire very close. I hid behind my truck and kneeled down trying to locate the shooting. Meanwhile, there were still shots being fired close by. It turns out we had orders to each test fire our weapons into a large sand berm. We don't have a radio in

---

our truck so I thought we were under attack. After I knew what the hell was going on I walked over to the ditch and fired a round into the dust about fifty yards away. I can't believe how crazy this place it.

I'm test firing my weapon somewhere in Iraq,
MSR (main supply route) Tampa.

Live Fire in Iraq

Driving the unfinished road in southern Iraq called Tampa was brutal. There was almost ninety miles of unpaved road that was pure dust and all bumpy. I hated that stretch of road because you couldn't relax as you were flying out of your seat constantly. The dust from the trucks in front of you, or passing you, headed back into your windows and stuck to your clothes because of the sweating you were doing. Most of the time the truck ahead of you would disappear into a cloud of dust and you had one of two choices. One was to keep your speed and just hope you didn't hit the truck in front of your if it had stopped or slowed down or two, was to slow down until the dust cleared and drive out of the preceding dust cloud. I chose the second way because there was no way I was going to die in a truck accident in a combat zone. To be killed by the enemy was out of my hands, but to die because I'm playing some macho role and too embarrassed to go slow was not for me. There were times that trucks behind me would get impatient and pass me, just compounding the problem by raising more dust. I remember once, the truck behind me passed me, and the passenger yelled at me to speed up and follow him. As soon as he got a few feet in front of my bumper, he disappeared into the familiar dust cloud. I had to laugh because it was impossible to follow him because I couldn't see him. Once, while we were on a wide stretch of the road, the truck behind us tried to pass. My driver sped up because we were in a clear spot and there were no dust clouds in front of us, just clear sailing. So, now there are two seventy-ton trucks side by side trying to get ahead of each other. Then alongside the second truck comes another, and finally, another. There were four HETs side by side racing down a sandy, bumpy road in a combat zone called Iraq. I yelled at my driver to "slow the fuck down" but he wasn't going to let the others get by us in the dust. This went on for a while, and the whole time I couldn't believe the stupidity of the situation. I didn't give a shit if the cargo we were carrying ever got where it was suppose to get, but I sure as hell wanted ME to get where I was going eventually and that is HOME! So much for convoy safety and integrity. Another time we stopped and got out to pull security as usual. I stood in the dusty sand, covered in sweat, rifle on my hip, locked and loaded, staring out into nothingness. All of a sudden a soldier opened fire with his M-16. He walked up to a sand berm and kept shooting down into a hole on the other side. I quickly hid under part of my truck and raised my rifle ready to shoot. My driver and I looked at each other and wondered what the hell was going on. Then the whole convoy opened up. Everyone was shooting into the berm along the road. My driver and I still didn't know what anyone was shooting at, but we thought we were under attack. I remember looking for targets but finding none, so we held our fire. Then the convoy commander came up to us and told us to test fire our weapons into the berm. It seems that the convoy was test firing their weapons in case we hit an ambush up the road where ambushes have taken place the past couple of days. The only trouble was that no one had told us about the stop to test fire the weapons. We each stepped out from under the trucks protection and fired our weapons. I had finally fired my rifle in Iraq and it was into a pile of sand. Communication was always a problem with our convoys in Iraq. Almost every convoy got lost at least once per mission, and most times we had no idea why we would stop, or why we would do anything. Just follow the truck ahead of you and hope for the best.

Previous letter home continued

I've kept my flak vest on all day. It's soaked through with sweat right now. I also kept my helmet on all day and held onto my good luck charms. Once in awhile I ask your good luck charms to bring me luck. So far, so good. I love both of you tons.

Saturday It's 0540 and I'm getting up at the Baghdad Airport. I slept at the back of the trailer.

I awake to another wonderful day in Iraq.

It was a warm night at the beginning but got cooler later on. Helicopters and planes were taking off all night. We slept right next to the runway. It was surprising how I could sleep through all that noise. I was really tired last night. I heard some artillery go "boom" through the night. Every night as I lay on my cot I look up at the stars. They are always out because there are never any clouds. I think of you both as I'm looking at the stars and wonder what you are doing. I love both of you very much and miss you a great deal. I hope we get sent home soon because this war is getting me down and I need to get back to normal.

I'm drinking the orange/ pineapple powdered drink you sent me. I like it and so do all my buddies. That was a good move.

We're off to an air base somewhere by the Syrian border (turned out to be Pecan Air Base between Fallujah and Ramadi). I'll touch my good luck charms from you all day and ask you girls for "luck." I love you both like crazy!

10:30 AM You are not going to believe this one! First, we're lost just ourside the Syrian border in a large city. We were making a U-turn in the sand, of course, and the lead vehicle got stuck. So, now we have tied up traffic in this town and have a major fucking mess (the town was Ramadi). While we drove through the town, people mostly were waving and friendly, but a few gave us the thumbs-down or yelled, "Fuck you." One time while we were stopped in the town, which is a no-no, about five or six little girls were on the corner waving at us. I waved back and did the thumbs-up. We waved back and forth for about five minutes. It was very cute.

3:10 PM What a fucking day! While we were stuck in the city (Ramadi) we had the entire section of town at a standstill. There were hundreds of cars stopped.

I ended up directing traffic. One car came toward me the wrong way so I lifted my rifle at him. He turned around and left. What an asshole! I was nervous the whole time because I was afraid someone would take a shot at me and I would have never known. I had my rifle at the ready the whole time motioning people to move over. It was such a mess. Also, it was a bad area. It was strange. I was excited, adrenalin pumping, and scared the whole time. To think I'm standing in a crowded street in a war zone in a city where most of the people hate us. I want to come home.

Fallujah and Ramadi

Another mission. Left Baghdad International Airport (BIAP) and headed to Pecan Air Base west of Baghdad. This was the first time going in this direction toward the Syrian border for me. Passing through Fallujah was typical of any town. Tons of men and boys on the streets, in the markets, but mostly just standing around selling their sodas, lamb meat, ice, and a million other things. Fallujah was a mean place for Americans. Going through we passed Bradley Fighting Vehicles and Abrams Tanks all along the road as they were pulling security. At one point there was a Bradley with it's main gun pointed right down the road, at us! I remember a soldier on his hands and knees going through a pile of sand in the road. He was uncovering a IED (improvised explosive device). My battle-buddy, who was driving, and I drove right next to that soldier not even thinking of the fact that if that bomb went off, not only would that soldier be killed, but our truck and us would go up with it. I remember the tanks parked under some palm trees just off the road pointing their main guns toward the road, toward the people, and toward the town itself. This was the most heavily guarded road and town I had been to except for the Baghdad Airport. We crossed a bridge over the Euphrates River. MPs were holding up all the civilian traffic so our HETs could get through. I was right in the middle of all this and yet I was just staring at all the action as if I were watching a movie. The only difference was that I had a locked and loaded M-16 pointed out the window. We continued on the road when my driver and I spotted planes parked to the right of the road. We figured that was Pecan Air Base, yet our convoy continued past and kept rolling toward the town of Ramadi. As we entered Ramadi it looked like all the other towns. People, mostly men and boys, walked everywhere, cars sped out of the driveways and side roads, dirt patches, and garbage surrounded our trucks. The civilians drove like they had no fear of our trucks despite the fact that we were the largest trucks in the Army's inventory and weighted seventy tons plus and we could take out a car without even feeling a small bump. Raising my left hand to the wire that blows the air horn was how I let them know that I was coming through and I was not slowing down. To stop in a town was the worst thing that could happen because then you become a stationary target. Our convoy had gone through almost the entire town when we stopped. Everyone had to get out of the vehicles and pull security by standing next to the trucks with our weapons at the ready. I stood at the front bumper on the driver's side. Helmet strapped on, flak vest done up, and wearing just a t-shirt because it was another day over 120 degrees, I stood and watched. People started coming out of every side street and building to see the Americans. Adult men, young boys, and little girls, but no women. Several people tried to speak to me and I smiled and looked back at them, having no idea what they were saying. A small crowd started to gather around me, so my team leader sent my battle-buddy to my side to cover me. He was getting a little nervous at the crowd I was attracting. Finally, the convoy loaded up and we were on our way again. People were out on their balconies, all over the sidewalks, and even in the road as we drove off. We arrived at a bridge at the northeast part of town and found out our trucks were too heavy to cross it. As the lead truck in our convoy turned around alongside the road leading up to the bridge, it got stuck in the deep, loose, powdery sand that is everywhere in Iraq. There was a large cement wall on one side of the stuck truck and the road on the other side. Because it was the lead truck, it blocked the rest of the convoy from moving as all the other trucks had started to make the turn behind it. At this point we had blocked the entire road except for two lanes leading toward the bridge. There were a group of soldiers around the stuck truck all giving directions on how to get the truck out. The wheels just kept digging into the loose sand. Traffic was not a total fucking mess. We had gridlocked the north part of the town of Ramadi. One of our trucks, which was called LMTV or Light, Medium Transport Vehicle, which we called the LMNOP Truck, was now blocking traffic off the bridge coming in our direction. We were trying to get the convoy back onto the road that we had just driven through the town on. It turned out that it wasn't because the bridge couldn't hold our vehicles, rather we had passed the Pecan Airbase like my driver and I thought earlier. Now we needed to retrace our route. There were four lanes of traffic heading east toward the bridge that we had to narrow down to two. One soldier was out in the road by himself trying to get that accomplished. I got out of my truck and steeped into the street to help him, which began my scariest moments in Iraq. As I stood in the street, I felt scared and excited at the same time. I had my M-16 at the ready, and with my left arm I was waving the cars over as they came around the curve toward the bridge. The cars were stuck in the traffic jam that we had created and passed slowly by me, sometimes stopping right next to me. I would look into the windows and see all of their faces looking back at me. Little children would stare or sometimes wave. I'd wave back to the kids. The adult men looked at me mostly with hatred in their eyes. I kept wondering which one of these men was going to pull a gun out and shoot me dead in the middle of the street. I watched very closely at every car that passed or stopped next to me. I was scared shitless every second I stood out on that road, yet I proved to myself that I could do what I had to do in a dangerous situation. This was one of the defining moments of my life. One car had gotten around the truck that was behind me and was blocking the traffic from coming in the opposite direction. As he approached me I raised my weapon and pointed it right at the driver. He stopped, smiled, and turned around. I often wonder how much closer I would have let him get to me before I opened up on him. Would I have? I was ready to with my finger on the trigger, but I guess I'll never really know. After about a hour or so in the street in Ramadi, we got the truck unstuck and went back through the town. As our convoy started down the main road through Ramadi, we stopped again and had to pull to the side of the road. Several of our HETs passed us after a few minutes, and my driver and I became the last truck in the convoy. The last truck is the one you don't want to be because that was the truck the Iraqis were targeting at this time of the war. At the beginning of the war they would hit the lead truck, but that brought all the fire power of the remainder of the convoy on their asses. They got smarter and started hitting the last truck. We were it! This made me even more nervous than normal. The convoy drove for a short distance and stopped again, right in the middle of town again. Immediately we were surrounded by people again. There were a lot of children, so we felt a little safer. When the children disappear it's usually a sign that something bad is going to happen. But, since we were practically surrounded by children, we relaxed a little. I only had one pack of candy left as I usually threw candy out the window of my truck to the kids as we drove through towns. There was one very cute little girl about five years old in a red dress in a crowd of about fifteen kids. Every time I tried to hand her the candy through the truck window, the older kids would crowd her out. After about five tries to give the girl the candy an Iraqi man came up to the truck and gestured he would give the girl the candy. I held back and asked him if he understood that I wanted the girl to have it. He shook his head yes and I handed him the bag. He handed it to the little girl and she skipped off down the sidewalk with the biggest smile saying, or singing, words I didn't understand. This was the best moment I had in Iraq. That little girl skipped away with my heart that day. In the middle of terror and misery I had a moment of sheer happiness. The convoy then headed back toward Fallujah and Pecan Air Base. Rifle pointed out the window, locked and loaded, I left Ramadi and the day I experienced both fright and accomplishment at an extreme depth.

Letter home continued

I love you both and can't wait to be with you both again.

Thank goodness for the kids. They wave. The little girls are the best. They wear little dresses and are so cute. I throw them candy as long as there are no boys around because they'll take it. They call us, "Mister, Mister." Cute.

I love you two!

7:55 PM The end of the day was great! First we had to drive back through the same town we weren't suppose to be going through in the first place.

We made it to the air base called Saddam Air Base. We have no planes here. There are blown up enemy jets and bombs and rockets all over the place. It's surreal.

Then after we unloaded all our equipment we went, and get this, swimming in a lake! It was guarded by two 50cal machine gun nests on the hills and enclosed by barbed wire so the Haggis can't come in our swimming area with their boats. The lake is huge and fucking warm like bath water, but it felt great! We swam and played and talked and I had a smile on my face the whole time. I took a couple of pictures.

I'm finally smiling!

Now we are on the base, cots set up on our trailers, ready to go to sleep. It has been one hell of a day! I love you guys!

Wild Dogs

Pecan Air Base, west of Fallujah. We brought some engineering equipment up from Kuwait to the airbase. We finally arrived after getting lost driving through Ramadi and a few hours of tension with a stuck HET in the northern part of the city. We unloaded the vehicles and found out there was a lake nearby. Part of the lake was inside the perimeter of the air base, and knowing this, we immediately wanted to be there. The temperatures had been over 120 degrees every day that we had been in Kuwait and Iraq on this mission. We piled into the back of a LMTV (light, medium truck vehicle) and were off to the lake. We had to wear our helmets because it's a theater wide rule to wear them while inside a vehicle. So, here we were, about twelve of us, sitting on the benches in the back of a truck in shorts, no shirts, boots on, and helmets. A funny sight to be sure. After a few minutes, someone lowered the back flap of the canvas cover, and we took our helmets off because no one could see us inside the truck. Peeking out of the corner of the canvas flap, we passed blown up Iraqi jet fighters and saw piles and piles of bombs and missiles just lying out in the open. It seemed very strange to see all those explosives just lying in the open. We finally pulled into a parking lot, and as we lifted up the back flap, there it was. A lake! An actual, full of water, lake. As we got out of the back of the truck, we walked toward the water. There was a large tent off to one side for people to change into shorts if they were wearing their uniforms, which none of us were. We left whatever things we brought with us inside the tent and headed for the water. Two things stood out before we even walked into the water. One was the barbed wire that was out in the water surrounding the area where we were to swim. The reason for the wire was to keep out Haggis in boats from approaching us while we swam. The other odd thing was a 50 cal machine gun nest up on top of a hill overlooking the swimming area. Not your average swimming hole, but we didn't care. We had water to swim in on a hot Iraqi day. I was so excited to be going into the water I could hardly wait to get there. I had been suffering greatly because of the heat that tortured me daily. As I walked into the water I was immediately disappointed. The water was the temperature of warm bath water. I stood there knee deep in the water yelling, "Can't anything in this shitty country be cold?" But, realizing that it was still better than anything else we had going that day in Iraq, I plunged in with the rest of the guys. The only way to get cool was to get totally wet and then stand up so the warm breeze would blow over your skin. In this way you could feel a slight coolness. The air conditioning effect. We swam around for a couple hours, laughing and just relaxing for a change. Some people wrestled, some raced, but most of us just squatted down and stood up over and over to feel the coolness of the breeze over our wet skin. It was a great break in a hot war. After a while we headed back to our HETs to get ready for the night at Pecan Air Base. We drove our HETs from the spot where we had dropped off the engineering equipment to a spot on the tarmac near the showers and mess hall. The mess hall was just a trailer set up with food cooked in cartons that tasted like cardboard. Supper was lousy, but showers awaited us in the tents off to one side. We put up our cots and got everything ready for the night, then headed for the showers. After the showers we settled down on our trailers with our cots and just sat around talking. It always amazed me that we could be in a huge open area, like the tarmac on the Pecan Air Base, and not feel any breeze. It was hot, and there was no wind. When darkness fell people laid down to rest for the night. That's when the wild dogs started their nightly howling and stalking. Everywhere we went in Iraq there were wild dogs. They would howl all night and wander around our trucks. Pecan Air Base was the worst place for wild dogs that I experienced. They started howling before dark and kept it up for most of the night. As the night wore on the dogs got closer and closer and louder and louder. There was a point in the night that I wanted to grab my M-16 and start shooting at them. They were robbing me of my sleep and I didn't get too much sleep on a mission. In the early morning when we woke up, you could see the paw prints of the wild dogs all around our trailers. They had quieted enough to get close and see what scraps we had dropped on the ground. The wild dogs in Iraq looked a lot like the domesticated dogs we have here in the states, except they always appeared to be smaller, and they were always dirty. I once saw a soldier feeding a wild dog and petting the dog, but I never let them get close to me. There was enough to worry about in Iraq without getting bit by a wild dog and worrying about what disease it might be carrying. We packed our gear, loaded it up, and left Pecan Air Base for BIAP and another mission. I was sweating before it was 0800 and I cursed the sun and the lousy country I was in.

The view out my front window as I drive down the road.
It's hot, sunny, and sand blowing, like always.

Previous letter continued

Sunday, 6:45 AM. I just got done eating breakfast and taking a shit in a Vietnam style shitter. The kind where they burn the shit with diesel fuel. I took a picture of the burning shit in the can because no one would believe me if I didn't.

Posing in front of the shit can.

Last night was a nice one. Laying in my cot under the stars. Just a little too warm, but not bad. As always, I thought of you two and wondered how you are and what you were doing. The weirdest part was I felt very peaceful. I'm not sure why. Maybe because of the scary day I just lived through, or whatever.

We'll be taking off for a base called Anaconda, north of Baghdad about 60 miles. What today has in store for me, I don't know. We'll see. I love you both like crazy!

10:30 AM. We're at Anaconda. Four trucks are picking up loads. I'm hoping that's all there is because we're not one of the four. This is the base that got mortared (bombed) the last time we were here so we want to load and leave for a safer base.

I sure feel sorry for the females in this part of the world. I see them working their asses off carrying large loads of straw on their backs, or working in a small pond piling up salt, or whatever. And the men are standing around yakking. I hate this place and feel true sorrow for any girl born here. They start out so innocent and end up in a dead end life.

Females in Iraq

As I drive down the roads in Iraq, there is something about the people that catches my attention. When we drive through towns there are almost no women walking around. Only men and boys everywhere. The men are mostly dressed in all white with either robe-type clothes or regular pants an shirts. The boys are dressed in mostly pants and shirts. They are everywhere. Selling things, walking across the road between our trucks, standing, talking, or just staring at us as we pass by. Some of the men just look, some give us the evil eye, some yell things at us that I can't hear or understand, some give us the finger, and once in a while one will grab his crotch while yelling. It didn't take them very long to learn the "finger" salute that we use. When I first arrived in country I waved as most people waved back. I had a smile on my face as well as most people we passed. After just a few weeks everything changed. No longer were we friendly toward each other. I started yelling out the window, "Fuck you!" and waving my middle finger at them as I yelled it. My rifle was always pointed at them, and near the end I was praying that one of them would do something so I could shoot him. In a matter of days I went from happy to be in Iraq helping the people to wanting to shoot one because I hated them so much. I mostly noticed the women in the fields as we drove through the countryside. They either had large bundles of sticks or hay or grass on their backs, or they were bent over in the ponds along the roads piling up salt so that when the water evaporated they could harvest the piles of salt. They were always surrounded by kids. They were near their homes. They were always working. The men were always standing around.

*A typical street scene in Iraq. One of the men in front
doesn't like us much.*

I used to tell the other soldiers that if we just gave every house a TV and
hooked them up to cable, maybe they would stop trying to kill us and
watch TV to pass the time. No one ever took me seriously even though I
still think that may have been the answer. The one part that stood out was
that the women had to wear black clothes. The men wore white and the
women wore black. It was over 120 degrees every day the summer of 2003,
and I couldn't understand how they could be in dark colored clothes. I was
miserable in my DCUs (desert Camouflaged uniform). To me, this was one
example of how "second class" the women were treated in Iraq. I noticed in
the cities that the women walked behind the men. They carried the loads of
whatever while the men just walked without having to do any work or carry
any load. Sometimes the women, while waiting along the road for a ride,
would turn their backs to us as our convoys passed by. I realize that certain
cultures have different ways of doing things, but it seemed to me that this
culture was wasting half of their population's talents by keeping them down
and treating them as if they were slaves. The little girls were always the best
sight. While they were young they were allowed to wear dresses that had
color. They would run up to the road and motion to their mouths that they
wanted food, and my heart would melt. I always tried to have candy to throw
to the girls. Then at about the age of ten or so, they seemed to disappear
into the black clothes and weren't noticed. I did see a limited part of Iraq
by keeping to the roads of the country. Only a few times did we actually go
through a city, and they were Fallujah, Ramadi, and southern Baghdad early
on in our time in-country. There were so many cities at which we traveled

the outskirts where there were markets and selling booths along the way. My impression of the men was that they didn't do anything but stand around and sell things and talk. The women always were with the kids or working in the fields or near the home. As an American, used to the American way of life, I had a hard time watching the way women were treated in Iraq. I had the distinct feeling that they were treated as slaves and not as people with equal abilities and intelligence of men. It was hard to think of the cute little girls growing up into the black robes and the life without hope of being able to enjoy the same freedoms as the men seem to have.

Previous letter continued

This Anaconda Base is another one of Saddam's air bases. Here is how crazy this guy was. He hid his jet fighters, MIGS, on roads outside of the air base. I could see them as we entered the base. What good they did there is beyond me. I guess he was trying to hide them. Why didn't he use them?

I saw a lot more blown up tanks and stuff today. There were places where there must have been some major battles.

The air base we came from had a huge crater in the middle of the runway. Actually, it was right where two runways crossed. We blew the shit out of this country.

Well, we're going to fuel up our trucks and get ready to go to Camp Cedar. It's close to Kuwait and it will get hotter. The difference in temperature between Kuwait and Baghdad is about twenty degrees. It only gets to about 110 degrees here. Yikes! That's still too fucking hot! I love you both like crazy.

Oh yeah, while driving through town a guy held up his shoe, which is suppose to be a great insult, so I gave him the finger. I hate the men here. I am positive I could shoot one and not lose any sleep.

I love you two and want to hold you forever!

1:35 PM Still at Anaconda. We were supposed to be on our way but there a foul-up, as usual. I'm in the truck just sitting in a dusty, sunny place sweating my ass off. What's new?

Story time. Yesterday, when we were stopped in town, there were about ten children around my truck. There was one little girl, about five years old, in a red dress, dark hair and a pretty face. I only had one pack of candy and I wanted her to have it. I would point at her, and she would raise her arms, but every time I tried to give the candy to her all the other kids would crowd her out. So, I got an older man to give it to her. As soon as she got it she ran, skipping down the sidewalk, squealing. It was perfect!

I wish I could have gotten someone to take a couple pictures of me out in the street directing traffic yesterday in Ramadi. It's going to be hard to explain to people that time here. Even today it's hard for me to believe what I was doing in such a dangerous place. I don't mean to scare you two, but it was really nuts.

I have felt pretty good on this mission. I have an appetite again as it came back about three weeks ago. And, I seem to be able to work pretty good. I just get a headache every day. No big deal. I'm trying very hard to drink a lot of water.

I'm not really sure what we, as a nation, are accomplishing here. It seems so futile. Hopefully, it won't be my problem too much longer. I love you both soooo much! 4:30 PM We have moved from one part of Anaconda to another part. I tried to walk to chow but it was too far and too fucking hot so I turned back. I got another headache. Damn, I'm tired of being hot and the sun shinning all the time. I would love to stand in a heavy, cool rain right now.

Not much new. I'm just waiting to see where we will sleep tonight. I'll think of you both and miss you both. Did I mention I love you?

Mortars, Flares, and Stars at Camp Anaconda

Lying on my cot in Camp Anaconda north of Baghdad. Unloaded during the day at BIAP and am picking up vehicles at Anaconda. We're staying in the middle of the camp because last time we were camped at the back edge of the camp a mortar round went over our heads and hit an Iraqi fuel truck, injuring the driver. The cot is on the trailer out of the sand. My battle-buddy has his cot near the front, and I'm at the rear hoping for a breeze. The cot is placed just so because there are holes in the trailer for tying down equipment and grooves that are uneven for other purposes. The cooler is near with a roll of toilet paper, my flip-flops, my water spray bottle, my camera, my helmet, flak fest, and rifle. I'm in a pair of Marine shorts that are thin, for coolness, and very short. The guys tease me about them all the time, but over here I don't give a shit because it's all about trying to stay cool. It's hot as always, so I'm just lying on top of the cot, no covers. The outer layer of the sleeping bag is piled underneath in case a miracle happens and I actually get cool, which usually happens about 4 AM or so in Iraq. I have a small camouflaged pillow that I bought at Camp Roberts back in California. It's so dirty, it's stiff, but I use it on the missions because everything is dirty out here on the road. My uniform is hanging on the ramps of the trailer airing out from the day's sweat. My boots are underneath the cot but at the end away from my head because they smell from the day's heat and sweat, too. There are no clouds, as usual during the summer nights, and the stars are out. Every night as I look at the stars I think of my girls back home and feel a certain peace come over me. Somehow it connects us. It's the only time I feel at peace in this shitty country. Once in a while a flare goes off and floats back to earth. Sometimes there are two or even three at a time. As I

---

lay in the cot I think about mortars. I wonder if I will see the black shape of the shell as it comes toward me before it blows me to hell. I sometimes can picture the dark shadow in the sky. Mortars are so random. Life in Iraq seems random. Nothing makes sense. I'm here to help and the people are trying to kill me. Then I fall asleep and leave the nightmare of life in Iraq for escape of sleep. It's the opposite here. The nightmare begins when you are awake. The peace is when you are asleep.

Previous letter continued

Monday How do I explain today to someone who isn't here? We left Anaconda at 8 AM. The worm has turned for me. I've gone from waving to giving people the finger. If they wave to me, I will wave back. But, if they give me the thumbs-down or show me their shoe bottom I will give them the bird. I hate this fucking country and their fucking people. They are killing and wounding soldiers daily, so I say, "Fuck 'em!"

Driving Through Towns

As I drive my HET through town, any town in Iraq, it's always the same. We close up as much as possible for our huge trucks and stay on each other's bumpers. In the states we are trained to keep our intervals and watch our speed and all that bullshit. But here in Iraq we stay as near to the ass end of the vehicle in front of us and go as fast as possible through the towns. To slow down makes you an easier target. To spread out makes you an easier target. To stop is to tempt fate. So, the person in the shotgun seat tightens their grip on their weapon, and the driver hunches over the wheel with a little more tension.

Driving through a town in Iraq.

The first thing that happens is that traffic picks up. Cars come out of driveways, other roads, and just out of nowhere. They crowd your truck and cut in front of you, and there is no order to the madness. There are no street signs, no stop signs, no lights, nothing to try and put a little order into the chaos.

A typical street scene in Iraq. No rules!

I don't slow down. If a car or van or bus comes close to my truck, I may swerve a little, but I don't take my foot off the gas, and I don't ever give way to an Iraqi vehicle. If they get too close, and many did, we hit them. Our trucks are so large that we barely feel anything as we destroy their car, or just their fender, or door, or whatever. No matter what we keep rolling. As the crowds grow the people start staring at us as we pass. Some wave, mostly the kids, and some give us the finger, and some of the younger males will throw rocks at our trucks. Some just stare with hate in their eyes. Once in a while, when a woman is present, she will turn her back to our trucks. When we enter the center of the town and there are people lining the streets, they start to cross between our trucks. They act as if we can't hurt them. I have come within inches of killing an Iraqi with my truck just because they needed to cross a street and we didn't slow down. I always kept my hand on the cord that blew the air horn because that was the only warning they would get from me to "get the hell out of the way." The Haggis seem to have no concept of parking out of the way either. They would pull their car out in front of you and then park it right in the road. There were times that we would be driving down the road in town only to have a car come at us on the wrong side of the road. It was as if they thought they couldn't be hurt or killed if we struck them. When we went through the downtown part our trucks were about the level of the second story. I could see right into the rooms over the street and watch the people on their balconies. Everything seemed so dirty and brown and covered with sand. Cloth hung everywhere for drapes or doorways. There were narrow islands in the center of most towns and people would stand on them as we passed within inches of them going thirty to forty miles per hour. It all seemed so bizarre. Once, as we were passing a couple hundred civilian fuel trucks, they just parked along side the road. Not in a line, rather just anywhere. They were two and three deep sticking out into the road. I had to drive up over a curb in the middle island to pass some of them. One of our trucks didn't get over enough and hit a fuel truck. It ripped a large gash in the underbelly of the tank, and fuel started pouring out all over the road. Needless to say, the Haggis jumped into their trucks and started pulling them over as far away from our passing trucks as they could. When a convoy of thirty or forty HETs are coming through, it's a pretty impressive sight. I have seen trucks run over guard rails, hit cars, jump over curbs, tear down roadside stands that were too close to the edge of the road, and hit just about anything else that we encountered. After the first month in-country almost none of our trailers had tail lights or fenders anymore because of us hitting things. I have seen one of our trucks take down the guard shack on the Kuwait and Iraq border. I have seen one of our trailers go over a cement barricade like the kind we would see at a construction site here in the states. I have seen one of our trailers swing out on a turn and push a brand-new looking car over two lanes into another van. The truck that did it hardly knew it had hit anything. I once ran over a dog that had run out into my path. I never felt a thing and only after we stopped and driver of the truck behind me said, "Man, you massacred that dog back there. It must have hit all forty wheels." did I know I had killed it. My first kill in Iraq and I didn't even know I did it. There were times that I don't know how I missed hitting and killing an Iraqi. Once, barreling through one of the towns, a car of about six men pulled right in front of my truck and then slowed down. I don't know why I bothered but I had to stand on the brakes to keep from running over that car from behind. I wonder if those idiots ever knew how close I came to smashing them to Allah or if they were just fucking with me. Every drive brought adventure. No two drives, or days for that matter, were the same in Iraq. To this day I will never understand the Iraqis and their disregard for their own safety when it came to our trucks. If I was on a road somewhere and a fifty ton truck that was almost two stories high came down the road, I would sure as hell get out of the way.

I'm riding down a road in Iraq, rifle pointed out the window,
locked and loaded.

Previous letter continued

I drove over ninety miles of bumpy, dusty, unpaved road during a sandstorm today. There were several times I had to come to a complete stop because I couldn't see anything in front of me. Imagine one hundred Army trucks passing each other, dusting each other, while the sandstorm blows. You bounced the whole time so much that all your bags fall off their perch, rifle slides in your lap, and after a while, both knees ache from the pounding. One of the most frustrating and dangerous things I've ever done.

I can't describe how tired I am, hot, smelly, unclean, and how weak I feel now. I hope I can get some sleep tonight.

I miss you so much and love you both more than I can write in words. I want to come home.

Tuesday The night was cool and clear and great sleeping weather except for the drunk on the next truck over, who puked in his cot and the two outgoing rifle shots. Other than those two little items, no problem.

I can tell I'm becoming a veteran of this place. The rounds go off and I think, "Outgoing (that means our guys are doing the shooting)" or "It didn't hit anything." so I turn over and go back to sleep.

It's Ours

The day I knew I had been in Iraq too long occurred in the new Camp Cedar. Camp Cedar II was across the road from Tallil Air Base. Pulling

---

142

into the camp brought you down a dusty, partially unpaved road to the gate. Just inside the camp to the left was the DFAC, and farther north was the refueling point next to a giant area of fuel pods. We drove straight through to the back road that took us to the refueling point. Getting in line, waiting, moving up a little, waiting, and finally getting fuel, then to the parking area. The parking area for convoys passing through was in the southwestern side of camp. It was nothing but deep, powdery sand that rose up in clouds of dust as the huge HETs drove through to the parking lane. We lined up and parked in our lanes and shut down for the night. Cots were unloaded and put up. This was one place you wanted to be sleeping on the trailer if you could because the sand was so fine any movement made it rise into the air to settle on anything close by, especially sweating soldiers. Other convoys would pull in throughout the night despite the fact that no convoys were supposed to be out after dark. We were all covered by the dusty clouds of sand that rose up from the ground. Everyone was complaining and swearing at the new parked convoy after they dusted us. There was never an escape from the sands of Iraq. Earlier in the day we would be shuttled to chow in the back of a truck. The hot, long ride to chow was almost not worth it. After chow and after dark we would take our showers, either by water bottle or camping bag shower. There was a shower point on the base but it meant taking another truck ride and by the time you got back from riding in the back of the truck, you were covered with the powdery sand all over again. Then we settled down for the night. Some people would just sit and talk, others would go right to sleep, and still others would turn up their boom box and start drinking the beer or whiskey they had bought from the local Haggis outside the gate to the camp. The night I knew I had been in Iraq too long started with me on my trailer in my cot. Our trailers were empty as were on our way to pick up some equipment from BIAPS. I settled down and lay on the cot in my shorts. My water spray bottle was handy to spray myself every few minutes to help keep cool in the hot Iraqi night. I fell asleep after looking at the stars and thinking of my two daughters and wondering if I'd see the mortar shell that would come toward my head just before it killed me. I woke up to the noise of the drunk on the trailer next to me puking in his cot. He was so drunk that he just laid in his own puke and coughed for a few minutes. He had done this before so no one went to help. Everyone within earshot was just pissed off that he had woke us up with his puking. Besides, it was always odd that soldiers would get drunk on a mission in the middle of a combat zone. I never did. After the drunk was done puking and coughing he quieted down and I feel back asleep. The next thing that woke me up was a gunshot. I was instantly awake and listening for the action that usually followed a gunshot in Iraq. The next moment there was another shot in the dark. It was the sound of a M-16 being fired nearby. Since it was one of ours and outgoing I laid back down and went back to sleep. I knew it wasn't an AK, which sounds different from a M-16, meaning that we weren't being shot at; rather, one of us was shooting at one of the bad guys. So, back to sleep. The next day, as the drunk on the truck next to me was cleaning off his sleeping bag, I thought about how I reacted to the rifle shot in the night. I realized that I had been in Iraq too long. I wasn't as scared and nervous as I had been earlier on in my deployment and that meant I had changed. An afterthought about Camp Cedar II. On our way out of the camp on one of our missions my HET was parked just inside the gate waiting for the other trucks to line up. My battle-buddy and I spotted two wooden outhouses next to a few tents. We knew we had some time before the entire convoy lined up to leave, and knowing that it would be hours until we were someplace else we could shit at, we grabbed our toilet paper and headed for the shitters. We went into the Vietnam style outhouse with the half drum barrel underneath us and did our business. As we were coming out a couple soldiers spotted us from the tents and started yelling at us. They were telling us that those outhouses weren't in use anymore. We just kept walking to our truck and got in to wait again. As we sat there we watched the soldiers from the tents pull up some barbed wire and encircle the outhouses. I guess they really didn't want anyone else using their outhouses. My battle-buddy and I felt just fine leaving through the gate after having taken a shit in the "not in use" outhouses. Small pleasures are big deals in war.

Previous letter continued

I should be back at Camp Victory today after we drop off our loads in Camp Virginia. They are both in Kuwait.

I looked at the stars again last night and thought of you two as usual. Yesterday I hugged your "good-luck" charms tight with my hand. For a split-second I was hugging you two.

The guys are hoping we will learn something soon about going home. I know I am tired of it all, the heat, crappy food, warm water, danger, and missing you two. Maybe I'll have some good news soon.

I love you two like CRAZY!

Few facts about yesterday. We were supposed to get Hagi ice (can't drink it, but we use it to keep our water and soda cold), but didn't. I had nothing to drink for six hours except bathtub warm water. I just can't get that down. Without cold drinks this place is unbearable.

Thinking about swimming in that lake a few days ago and it seems like it never happened. Just a dream. I went back to the shit hole world so quick it seems like I just made it up.

Just sitting here ready to go to chow and hit the road. Should be back in Kuwait in about four hours. Did I tell you two how much I love you?

3:10 PM Back in Kuwait. It's about 130 degrees plus. It is cooler in northern Iraq. I forgot how hot it gets here in just six days.

Hours of boring driving today. Nothing but heat and desert. Northern Iraq is more dangerous but a lot cooler and more interesting.

I should be back in Base Camp Victory in an hour or so. Then I have to unload the truck, put my cot up, and pack my shit again. Never any rest for the warrior.

I sure hope I come home soon because I am very homesick and miss you two a great deal. I love you both.

Tidbits on the mission to Baghdad and beyond. My pants are so dirty I don't know if they will ever get clean again.

When we were in Anaconda there were flares going off in the night. I guess they were looking for some bad guys.

Lying down on a cot on a trailer under the stars can be relaxing after a day of boredom, excitement, and fear. That's when I think of you two the most.

I do a lot of sitting in the truck and waiting. It gets very boring sometimes.

I'm sitting, waiting, and sweating at BIAP.

There are only a few guys that I hang out with. The teacher, my battle-buddy, the guy I call "Mama Bear," and the young one. That's about it. Most of the rest are dumb asses I would never be around back home.

I love you two!

Riding to chow in the back of a truck with my battle-buddies.

5:30 PM I'm back safe. They are talking about a new mission tomorrow. Damn! No rest!

I love you both,

Dad

Trash

Everywhere you go, either in Kuwait or Iraq, there is trash. It's along the roadsides, in the fields, and piled alongside the houses and buildings. I remember laughing when I saw a sign in English in Kuwait that reminded people not to litter. As I looked around the sign there was trash everywhere. The people who put that sign up must have been drinking a lot that day because it was just too bizarre. I wish I could of taken a picture of that, but by the time I noticed the sign our truck was passing it. On our first mission we went through Basra. We weren't supposed to be there, but our fearless leaders had gotten us lost as they did many times. As we circled around to get back onto the road to take us back out of Basra I remember seeing piles of trash in every open spot in the city. There were pools of standing water filled with trash. There were piles of trash on top of piles of trash.

A street scene in Basra with trash everywhere.

I couldn't figure out how the people could live like that. They had just gone through a month of war in their country, so I guess they had an excuse. But after spending months in Kuwait and Iraq, the trash problem never got better. The people didn't seem to care. Whenever we would stop on our convoys, for whatever reason, no matter where we stopped there was trash along the road. I used to look closely at the trash to try and figure how it got there. I noticed a lot of the trash was boxes and bags from American MREs (Meals Ready to Eat, or as we called them, "Meals Rejected by Ethiopians"). But it wasn't all ours. There were wrappers of packages that I couldn't read. Iraq and Kuwait were just two countries with miles and miles of trash.

Posing by our HETs lined up at Camp Virginia, Kuwait.

I drove to Camp Doha, Kuwait to pick up some equipment. I'm sweating my ass off and these soldiers are swimming in the middle of the day. Unfair!

I'm pulling security while our convoy stops along a road in Iraq.

Showing my flag on my M-16.

First Trip to Doha, Kuwait

Camp Doha is near the water in Kuwait. After a couple months in-country, or in the "box," I had a chance to go to the large base camp there. Since I wasn't going on a mission, I took the opportunity to go to someplace different and get away from hot, boring Camp Victory where I just sat in the tent sweating and swearing. To go I needed to be in full uniform with helmet and vest. We were going in the back of an LMTV (Light, Medium Tactical Vehicle), or as it is know as, "the Army truck." There were about eight of us going to Camp Doha. The cover of the truck was rolled up on the sides. The temperature was unbearable. It was easily over 120 degrees. The sergeant in charge demanded that we keep our blouses (shirt) on the whole ride. I sat in the back of the truck sweating continuously and completely. I was miserable the whole ride. The driver of the truck was one of the worst drivers I have ever seen. He was going much too fast, and when he passed a car or truck, he would change lanes too quickly, shaking the bodies in the back like rag dolls. Once, he hit the brakes so hard that we all fell into each other as we were thrown toward the front of the truck. At this point I was yelling at the driver to "slow the fuck down." I kept thinking how stupid it would be to die in a combat zone in a truck accident because some moron didn't know how to drive. Now, I wasn't just sweating, but I was scared the truck was going to roll over and kill me. I was very relieved when we finally reached Doha. On the ride there I saw buildings that had no color and an actual big city. I think it was the outskirts of Kuwait City, but I'm not sure. It was just weird to see so many buildings that weren't blown to fuck after a couple months of tents and the battered towns of Iraq. Driving to the entrance to Camp Doha, I saw something I hadn't seen in months. Grass! It was beautiful and very out of place. We were unloaded at a parking lot about one-fourth of a mile from the PX (Post Exchange or the store). Just walking from the parking lot to the building was torture. It was even hotter at Camp Doha than it had been at Camp Victory. I could barely breathe. When I entered the building, there were small shops on one side, selling perfumes, clothes, souvenirs, and a uniform shop. There was a small donut booth that was empty of everything, and it was only about 10 AM. On the opposite side was the entrance to the PX. The biggest one I'd seen since leaving the states. But at the opposite side of the entrance was the prize. The food court. One end had a famous fried chicken stand, which had the longest line, an ice cream store, pizza place, and a sandwich shop. I went straight for the fried chicken line. The building was air conditioned, but I was still sweating like crazy. It took me a good twenty minutes to finally stop sweating. It took over one half hour to get my spicy chicken strips with barbecue sauce. Finding a seat was nearly impossible. You had to stand on the wall, wait for someone to get up, and race to the table, only to be beaten by someone closer or quicker. The soda with ice was perfect! I wanted the ice more than I wanted the soda in the drink. The chicken was the best! Those few minutes seemed worth the miserable drive in the heat in the dust. After eating I walked around and looked at the man across from the sandwich shop stand selling blankets. The last thing I wanted in the summer of Iraq and Kuwait was a blanket. A lot of people bought them, and I'm sure sent them home for souvenirs. There was a stand where a man was selling watches and other jewelry. Down the hall was a small USO room that had a TV in a smaller room where you could sit on a couch or chair and watch a movie. There were books to read and some tables and chairs so you could sit and read or write or even play a board game or some cards. I took some writing cards because they are good to send pictures through the mail in. Down the hall further was a library. The bad part about the library is that you couldn't take any bags or back packs in the library, and since I had a backpack, I stayed out. I wasn't going to leave it outside the door like some people did. Another large line was in the hall between the library and food court. It was the ATM machine. People were getting money and spending it. There were soldiers, and marines, and even some British soldiers. There were all different kinds of countries and units represented there. There were also a lot of WOMEN! Funny how after a few months in the desert of Iraq and Kuwait these women looked so sexy in a military uniform. I just sat at a table with a ice filled soda and stared at them for a long time. Although there are women in my transportation unit, seeing a lot of new women was quite a treat. After a while I went into the PX. It had everything I needed and more. It was quite a treat just to be able to be in a large store again. I walked around, looked at and bought a few things. One of my best buys there was a quart plastic bottle that had a twist off top. When I brought it back to my tent in Kuwait I would unscrew the top and cram it full of ice. I'd fill the remaining room with water and take it out when I had to work on the truck. I had cold water to drink instead of a bottle of water that would warm up too quickly in the desert heat. I didn't take it on missions because there was never enough ice on the road and most of the ice we got on missions in Iraq were bought from the Haggis. That water was tested by the Army and was found to have feces and urine and other junk in it. We only used Hagi ice to keep our drinks cold on missions. I spent the day looking at people, things, and enjoying being out of the heat. At 4 PM we had to meet the truck for the ride back. The same sergeant made us keep our uniform shirts on as we drove back. It was still unbelievably hot, and I was covered in sweat in no time. There was humidity around Camp Doha because of it's closeness to the water, so the heat was even more unbearable than at Camp Victory. By the time I got back I swore I wouldn't go again. It just wasn't worth the ride there and back in the heat. The same driver kept me scared of dying in an accident the whole way back. Mostly a miserable day, as usual, in this lousy war.

Letter home / 7-28-2003

Hi Girls,

I had to write to you about our new rumor. Today we are supposed to be on a list that says we will be leaving here in late August and home for good in September. Everything is starting to point toward it really happening. A few empty connex boxes arrived over the week end (they are the large containers that can be carried by truck, train, or boat). They were dropped off by our supply tent which could mean they will start packing soon.

The 3rd ID (3rd Infantry Division) is going home and when they do we are free to come home because that's the unit we are supporting.

So, it seems that this fucking nightmare is about to end.

When the plane touches down (wherever) if they are letting families be there (which they'd better) I want you two to be there. No excuses! If it's the airport near Sacramento you will have to drive, get a room (on me), and be there when I get off that plane because I am running to both of you and hugging you until someone forces me to let go. You both have to be there. Promise!

Remember to get your sleeping arrangements done before I get home. Get the place ready because Dad will be coming home soon.

Jennie, find out the best deal on a car under $10,000 so I can drive my car and you can have your own. Christie, you'll be next. You investigate where we need to get you to college for your music career.

I love you guys and can't wait to hold you again.

Dad

P.S. We must keep in mind that although this is a strong rumor, it is still a rumor.

Letter to school / 7-31-2003

Hey Everyone,

GET ME OUT OF HERE! This place is getting more dangerous than ever. The Haggis are hanging full soda cans off bridges now that will explode our windshields when they hit. They are also dropping Molotov Cocktails off the overpasses. So, we have been ordered to shoot anyone on a bridge. Yikes! I want to come home.

I leave for another mission tomorrow for somewhere in Iraq. Got our truck ready today with fuel, oil, etc. After this letter I have to pack my stuff for 6-8 days on the road.

Today is the last day of the month and I'm one day closer to coming home, whenever that is. There are rumors flying around and they all tell us we're leaving in August, but they are just that, rumors. We'll see. I'm ready to go now.

Any word on my teaching assignment for next year? It looks pretty certain I won't be home in time to start the school year.

Well, I'm OK, just hot and tired of these daily sandstorms. I'll be safe as I can because I want to come back and teach. I hope you are well and happy.

Joe

Letter home / Friday /8-1-2003

Hey Girls,

I'm sitting in the truck. It's 3:40 PM and we're waiting to leave on another mission to Iraq. We will stay in another camp here in Kuwait and then tomorrow head to Iraq. It's very hot today and another sandstorm. I'm riding with my teacher friend. He's really a cool guy and is very good at everything he does. I will keep notes

---

of this trip like I always do. Share it with Grandma. I will touch my good luck charms you two gave me every day for luck.

I love you and will think of you all the time.

After my phone call to you last night Christie, I kept thinking of home and you two girls. I got really homesick and couldn't sleep until after midnight. When I walked outside the tent the stars were out and like always it calmed me down and made me feel close to you. I don't know why looking at the night sky with the stars makes me feel closer to the both of you, but it does.

My Loneliest Night

I'm lying in the cot in the tent in Kuwait. It's hot, the lights are out, and people are sleeping, watching videos, or walking in and out of the tent over the plywood floor. The floor creaks and shakes your cot as people walk by. I've got my headphones on listening to music. Tonight the songs make me think of home and my daughters. I start to miss them more than usual. After trying to sleep I give up and walk outside the tent. The night is clear, stars everywhere. There are lights on in a distant motor pool. There are people out sitting on the cement bunkers smoking or just talking. People under the cammo netting at the entrance of the tent are sitting on cots or folding chairs. I stand just outside the cammo netting looking up at the stars and start to cry. I miss my daughters and feel lost in this shitty country. There is no end in sight to the madness of O.I.F., or Operation Iraqi Freedom. Every time we go out on a mission there are dangerous and miserable conditions. The downtime in Kuwait just gives you more time to miss home and the family. The skinny guy who's been sick comes out and asks me if I'm OK. I tell him I'm feeling homesick and he stands with me for a while. After a few minutes he walks away and I'm alone in the middle of thousands of people with my sadness and the stars. Through the dusty haze I can see lights in the background, cigarettes burning here and there, voices muffled that are all just background noise. I stand outside for about an hour feeling all the emptiness that being in a war halfway around the world from my home brings. Then I go back through the tent flaps, walk over the plywood floor and lay back down. Finally, sleep comes, but no peace. Just another end to another shitty day in a shitty part of the world in a shitty war.

Letter Continued:

I was sad when I called again and I didn't get a chance to talk to you, Jennie. But, it was nice talking to you, Christie.

Jennie, for Christie's birthday I told her she could have $200 for a guitar and whatnot. That's what you get for your birthday, too (the $200, not the guitar and whatnot).

Saturday / 8-2-2003

Well, the stars didn't come out until late last night so I didn't get a chance to look at them and think about you two. It was hot and windy last night. It was hard for me to fall asleep.

We've had breakfast and we're waiting to head out. We will go to the border of Kuwait and Iraq, which takes about three hours to drive, and then head into "bad-guy territory." We will stay at a camp called Cedar tonight. It should be cooler tonight for sleeping.

This morning there were hundreds of crickets all over the ground by our trailer. There was a wild dog going by, too. There are packs of wild dogs all over in Iraq. They howl all night and get closer and closer to our trucks as the night goes on. In the morning we can see their tracks around our trucks as they searched for food. More than once I have wanted to shoot one of them to shut them up.

It's hard to spend any time not thinking about home. I am very homesick and tired of this Army life. I hate the heat and I hate this fucking place. I love you both!

9:15 AM—We are getting close to the Iraq border. We stopped to buy some ice for our coolers.

It is hot! There is a breeze blowing and it's just hot air. I can see how people go nuts from stuff like this.

I used to think driving across Nebraska was the most boring drive ever but driving through the deserts of Iraq beat that by a mile. Just brown desert. No plants, no people, and nothing but hot fucking air.

I'm on the QRF (Quick Reactionary Force) for this convoy. It's the people who run to the trouble if there is any. Which is funny to me because if something happens everyone will be doing what they need to do. Not much sense in a QRF. The Army is weird.

Noon—We're at a place called NAVSTAR. It's just by the DMZ (Demilitarized Zone), outside the Iraq border. We got our briefing about how many ways the Iraqis are trying to kill us, which is a lot. We lock and load our weapons as soon as we cross the border. I'll be thinking of you and touching my good luck characters often. Here we go into Iraq. I love you both.

Navstar

After a couple hour drive from Camp Victory, Kuwait, there is a fueling point called Navstar. It is on the border of Kuwait and Iraq. This is the

"jump-off" point for convoys leaving Kuwait into Iraq. Our trucks don't need fuel so soon after leaving our base camp so we get our information and leave for Iraq. As you come into the entrance there is a cement divider like the kind they place end to end on freeways for construction. The corner is crumbled as if some heave vehicle had hit it, and just like everything in this part of the world, it's messed up. You turn into the small area. If there is a convoy ahead of yours, it's a slow process to get fueled up.

After getting fueled up you line up in rows. There are times you are the only convoy and there are times that the place is full of trucks from all different units. Once there were some Italians lined up nest to us headed north to Iraq. We were always there around noon and it was always hotter than hell. Just after the war started there were a couple guys outside the entrance sitting in a cement bunker keeping track of who entered. There was also a small store where you could buy some snacks and lukewarm sodas. After a couple of months they put a mobile building on the lot that was the operations center. We could go there for our briefing of what the latest news was on our convoy routes through Iraq. I used to try and be one of the first ones in the OPS so I could stand in front of the air conditioner. I would listen to how many ambushes there were yesterday on the road we were about to travel on, all the while standing in the back with the air blowing on my neck and head. I knew as soon as we left I would be back in the 120 degree plus heat for the rest of the day and night. Whenever we were around places like this we had to wear our blouse (the military name for the uniform shirt). I never understood why we had to "look good" while it was so hot. Picture yourself on a hot summer day at the beach and instead of lying on the blanket, you wrap it around yourself. Stupid! We always sat at Navstar longer then we needed to. Sitting in our trucks, the heat beating off the pavement, no air, sweating and sweating. Then the word to "load up" comes. Put the flak vest on, helmet on, and point your lock and loaded weapon out the window because is five minutes you will go through the DMZ between Kuwait and Iraq. You pass a station manned by the Kuwaitis that are stopping all the traffic entering their country, sometimes blocking the road so we can't get through. Then past a fence, a short area of sand, and another fence and you're in Iraq. The second you cross the border there is a sign warning you not to throw food to the people along the road. It threatens you with UCMJ (Uniform Code of Military Justice) action. We all ignore the sign and throw food to the children, who immediately run to the road when they see our convoy motioning with their hands to their mouths that they are hungry. It's a small town that we drive through and I only throw candy to the little girls that are without men or boys around. If there is a man or boy close by they will take the candy from the girl. There is one little girl who wears a hat that every time I go through and see her I make sure I have something special for her like a fruit cup or candy. Seeing her in a colorful dress that is caked in dust, bare feet, and a beautiful face breaks my heart every time. All the time I'm throwing candy out the window, one hand is on my weapon that I lay across the middle "dog house" (a large metal box between the driver and passenger of our truck), and my lap with the barrel out the window. I can only be sentimental for a moment because we've been shot at here before. It's still Iraq and they are still trying to kill us.

Letter continued

4:30 PM—We are at an air base called Tallil near Camp Cedar II. We filled up with fuel and are waiting for the other trucks to fuel up. It has been fucking hot today! It had to be 130 degrees easy. I haven't felt this hot in a few weeks.

You know how when a tire blows there are pieces of it all over the road? Well, we have to steer around those pieces because the bad guys are putting mines under them. This place is insane! Nothing exciting happened yet and I hope it doesn't. It's just so damn hot! I love you and think of you all the time.

6:30 PM—We're at the air base. I have my cot out on the back of our trailer. It is still very hot! I am so sick of being hot. I hope there will be few times that I am hot, or even warm, again. Be prepared for no heat this winter because I'm not roasting at night.

I'm eating MREs with my friends. Mine sucked!

We're parked in a dirt lot with all the trucks lined up. Not much to write about. More tomorrow. I love you both and miss you. I will look at the stars tonight and feel close to you.

Sunday / 8-3-2003

It's 5:50 AM. I slept like a rock. I was really drained. We head up to Baghdad Airport today. Then a little north to a place called Camp Anaconda. It's kind of cool right now but heating up fast. I going to go to chow, then we hit the road. The part of the road we will traveling on has ninety miles of unpaved, potholed, thick dusty sand. It's a bumpy, dirty, uncomfortable ride. That's how I'll be spending my morning.

No ice for two days now. I'll have to buy some Hagi ice this morning. "Hey Mista, Mista, one dollar, ice." That's what they yell at us as we drive by as they hold up a block of ice in a towel. It has traces of shit and piss in it so we have to rinse off everything before we drink whatever we're keeping cold with the ice. But at least it's cold.

I love you guys.

7:20 AM—I just got back from chow. They had watermelon and strawberry jam. I haven't had strawberry jam in months. It was so good I made three pieces of toast.

I had to load some ammo and water and food on a truck. Nice way to start a day. Off to Baghdad.

I love you two.

1:05 PM—We're fueling up at Scania. It will be my turn to drive now.

Scania, Fuel Point South of Baghdad

Driving up to Baghdad, or on the return trip from Camp Anaconda or BIAP, we usually stopped in a refueling point called Scania. It was just a place on the road where we pulled off into the soft sand and fueled up for the rest of the trip. The first few times we pulled into Scania, there was not much to see. Some fuel points, some tents, and some people that I felt sorry for because they had to live in this nothing place. After a few months, it was still a dump. One side of the road had the fuel points and the other built up with tents and more tents. I still felt sorry for the people who had to man this site. The first time we were there we would park on the road until the rest of the convoy got their fuel and then pull out as a group and continue on toward our destination for that day. As we were parked along the road waiting for the entire convoy to fuel up Haggis would come up to the trucks and try to sell us things. During the first missions they sold Iraqi money that was no good any more, a lot of bayonets, and some scopes, and other little things that we had no use for. As the war dragged on they started getting more things they found out we needed and would pay for. They started to sell coolers, which every truck bought at least two of, ice, a big seller because of the heat, sodas by the case, and flags, shirts, beer, and even hash (the smoking kind). After a while they started bringing in the whiskey, which was a big hit with a lot of soldiers. It was amazing to me that after we pulled into a camp for the night, yet were still in enemy territory getting mortared and shot at nightly, that some people would get drunk as hell. I had one beer on one mission and it got me goofy too quickly. It made my stomach so upset that it sent me to an outhouse in the middle of the night. I remember grabbing my flashlight and running to the nearest shitter. I was wearing my sleeping shorts and nothing else. I opened the door to the shitter and quickly squatted and let go a massive wet stream of shit over the opening. When I was finished I turned to clean myself and only then did I see that the seat to the shitter was closed. I had covered the seat cover with my shit. It was a fucking mess. So, I did what anyone would of done, I snuck out and went to the shitter next to the one I was just in, cleaned up, and snuck back to my truck. I even wiped out my foot prints in case anyone tried to track the asshole who shit all over the seat in the outhouse. I can imagine the outcome of someone opening up the door to that shitter the next day and seeing the mess I had left. I didn't want to be anywhere around when they did. When we first stopped along the road at Scania, the people would come right up to our doors as we sat inside of the trucks trying to stay out of the intense heat. Then more and more people starting dying by roadside bombs and ambushes, and we started dealing with the Haggis with one person keeping a loaded weapon on them while the other person did the dealing. There was a story going around that a truck driver was buying something from a Hagi and as the Hagi came up to the door to give the soldier his product, the Hagi pulled a pistol out from under the object and shot him in the face, killing him. After that story we started to be more careful. Sometimes the MPs would come flying up in their Hummer and point their 50 cal machine guns at them or their SAWs and yell at them to "get the fuck out of here" or "get your fucking asses out of here." I was amazed at how mean they were on my first mission, but after a while of being shot at and mortared, I didn't want to be nice to them either. After a few months they let some Haggis set up a little market place with barbed wire between us and the Haggis. On my last mission in country there was a line of merchants selling sodas, watches, coolers, ice, money, and a lot of other trinkets. One young guy, about twelve years old, had a lot of sodas to sell. I saw one case of strawberry soda and had to have it. But, over there it's expected to quibble about the price. He was asking eight dollars so I offered seven dollars. He wouldn't budge. This was not the way it usually goes. Seven dollars was the going price for a case of soda in Iraq in the summer of 2003. I walked away, playing hard to get, and returned in a couple minutes and offered seven dollars again, holding it out this time. He turned me down again. I walked away playing harder to get. We were about to load up and pull out so accepting defeat, I went back prepared to pay the eight dollars. I had checked everyone else's stand and couldn't find any strawberry sodas. When I got back to this kids stand, the strawberry soda was gone. So much for the fun of arguing over the price of an item. I left with something else from someone else but regretted not paying the extra dollar and having some great soda in the cooler for the remainder of the mission. That was one tough kid.

Shopping for soda at Scandia, Iraq.

Being in that abbreviated bazaar was the closet I've come to walking among the people of Iraq, except, of course, whenever we stopped in a town and had to pull security. People were coming back to their trucks from the bazaar with all kinds of things. One bought matching watches for himself and his wife. Others had their cases of soda. Others had stuff I couldn't imagine why they bought it. We loaded up and went on down the road in the heat. When we entered Scania from the south there were some Hummers under the bridge and on top was a bunker with a machine gun in it. Entering from the north there were some Hummers in the road and a bunker off to the side of the road with a machine gun in it. I'm sure there were borders to the side that were patrolled but I never saw them. I often wondered who was watching out for us from the sides. There were times you'd just drive in and fill up, and other times there would be one convoy next to another convoy with a long wait coming up. I remember once, while we parked alongside another National Guard Unit that some guys in another truck were laughing at what I had written on the side of my truck, which was "ONE WEEK END A MONTH, MY ASS!" I can't claim that saying as my own. I saw it on the side of a truck at BIAP once. But that's the only other time I had seen it on a truck, so I'm going to take some credit on spreading it around early in the war.

"One Week End A Month, MY ASS!"

One Week End A Month, MY ASS!

I was sitting in my HET just outside the Baghdad Airport. We were waiting for the convoy to get it's marching orders to Camp Anaconda north of Baghdad. We were waiting on the road that leads out into the city itself as this was early after the war supposedly ended, before that road became one of the most dangerous roads to travel in all of Iraq. There was a large noise wall next to our trucks that just kept any breeze from getting to us. It was hot again, no air, and the sweat dripped off my body. As I sat there with the door open and my feet up on the window ledge lying back in my seat, I was trying not to explode with anger at the fact I was so miserable. I watched as another convoy drove by in the opposite direction. As they passed slowly through the barricades that were everywhere to slow trucks and cars down should they be the enemy, I noticed on the side of one of the trucks some writing in chalk. It read, "One Week End A Month, MY ASS!" I immediately got it and laughed like I hadn't laughed in a long time. It means that when you sign up in the Reserves or National Guard they always tell you that it's "only one week end a month and two weeks of duty in the summer." Here I was in my sixth month of active duty and in the war in Iraq, and it was no fucking week end. I wrote that little saying on the side of my truck right there and then and kept it on my truck for the rest of my time in the box. I got several laughs as I went through check points, gates, or just had someone drive by my truck. I can't take credit for the saying getting all over Iraq, but I only saw that one truck with that sign, so I'll take some of the credit. When I was home months later I was reading the funnies in the newspaper one day and read a popular comic strip that is carried nationally. In the cartoon for that day was someone on a radio show talking to a National Guardsman. The soldier spoke of getting messed around with and not having the training for the war in Iraq, and then mentioned the new saying going around Iraq. He said that it was, "One Week End A Month, MY ASS!" Again I couldn't help but laugh because I was one of the troops that carried that sign across the shitty land of Iraq in 2003. The cartoon with a picture of my truck with the message on it as I point to it hangs in my house today.

Previous Letter Continued:

I still have a sad heart for the little girls here. They are so cute and yet so sad as they beg along the road for food and water. I know their life will be shit as they get older and I just want to scoop them up and take them home to save them. If we change that, the fact that women can live productive lives without the men dominating them, then being here is worth it. But, if it's only about the oil, then fuck it!

Very strange looking at everything in the road because it could be a mine. Very strange.

Too hot to write. I love you two.

6:40 PM. We're at the Baghdad Airport. We heard a convoy met some trouble on the way to the airport today so we were on edge coming in. Nothing happened to our convoy.

It was hot again, as usual. When we got to the airport our shitty leaders showed their weak-ass personalities. After sweating like pigs all day with our flak vest on, helmets on, in a hotter than fuck truck, some of us took our t-shirts off when we parked. Our leader came and chewed us out for having our shirts off and made us put them back on. What an ass! We do that every night on the road when we're parked in a camp or base.

Then, we haven't had any ice for two days and had to buy our own from the Haggis. Their ice is impure so we can't drink it, but we keep our pop and water cold. The rule is whatever base we're on has to supply us with everything we need, such as showers, food, and ice. Our leaders are too lazy and chickenshit to find out where it is and ask for it. Instead, they take up a collection to buy more Hagi ice. What a bunch of weakass people we have leading us.

I am so tired, physically and emotionally. I really need to come home soon. I'm tired of being scared and treated like shit.

It's fucking hot! Both of my ankles have scabs from scratching my flea bites, I have one pimple on each knee (go figure), an ingrown toenail that I'll have to cut open when I get back to base, cuts on my hands, and I'm sore everywhere. I really need to come home soon.

Thanks for letting me complain. I feel better. I hope I see you soon. I love and miss you both.

7:10 PM. I just took a shit on the ground between two connexes (big metal boxes that go on trains, boats, trucks, etc.). So, now I have shit at Saddam's International Airport, on the ground. It's a lovely fucking war! I love you two.

Monday / 8-4-2003 / 4:55 AM

I got up at 4 AM because I couldn't sleep anymore. My nose is clogged plus the helicopters that flew right overhead at about two hundred feet had a little to do with it. So, I took a quick shower from the camping plastic shower bag for $5 and cleaned up.

Last night was quite a night. The Haggis blew up a building here and then something with a lot of gas blew up and burned bright and long.

The first event was a building they blew up about 1000 yards away. I heard this big bang (WHOOOMP) and there was a big fire. After it burned down for a while I could tell it was a building on fire.

Then after about thirty minutes there was another explosion and a ball of flame shot into the air. It burned for about ten minutes and had to be a gas fed fire (it turned out to be a fuel truck).

I saw a few rounds go up and hit with a white flash. Then I could see tracers (bullets that glow at night) shooting up into the sky several times. It was at this time we were told to get our helmets and M-16s and keep them with us.

I sat up for a while talking with my battle-buddy about how crazy this place is and how nervous we are and how much we want to go home.

Mortar Attack at BIAP

Our trucks are parked on the south side of the runway in an open sandy lot with enough room for our large trucks. The tower is visible as well as a wrecked jet liner that was hit during the opening of the war. C-130s take off and land constantly. If they are landing they come in low over our heads and bank hard to their left coming in fast to land on the runway at Baghdad International Airport, or as we called it, BIAP. When they take off it's the reverse. They take off fast, bank to their right and climb as fast as possible. One plane, just during dusk, shot some flares out the back of the plane in a

defensive move. The cots are up, the cooler is filled with sodas and water and within easy reach. It's dark and I'm ready for sleep wearing only my shorts because it's fucking hot again. "WHOOMP!" A loud explosion is about 1,000 meters away and a building is on fire. I can tell it's a building that was hit even though it's dark because the fire is outlined in the windows as well as coming out the top. The building burns but there is no more action for now. A couple guys get their cameras out to try and take pictures with their flash and I tell them it's too far away, but they snap anyway. Then three more loud explosions hit close together in time and area. A huge ball of flame rises up hundreds of feet into the air. A fuel tanker has been hit. The fire burns bright and high for about five minutes. I climb to the top stair of the HET trailer to get a better view. It's then that one of my buddies yells at me to "Get the fuck down; we're being mortared, you idiot!" After I climb down a Bradley Fighting Vehicle goes rumbling by on the street next to where we are parked. A couple more go tearing by and they are in a hurry to get someplace. The word comes down that BIAP is on full alert and to get our weapons and stand by. I am dressed in my shorts, flip-flops, flak vest, helmet, holding my M-16 across my lap as I sit on my cot wondering what the fuck is going on. I'm feeling a little stupid sitting there in my outfit but I'm scared, too. I sit and talk with my battle-buddy as we listen and watch tracers being fired down range from somewhere on the airport. We talk about dying and how random mortars are. As I sat there talking and thinking about war I felt a great sadness for what was all around me. I watched the tracers go out from our lines into the night. Once in a while a flare of two would light up a section of the perimeter. The flames of the destroyed fuel truck burned out as well as the building. I couldn't tell you if someone put the fires out or they just burned themselves out. After about an hour things quieted down so I laid my rifle under my cot, placed my helmet and flak vest at one end of the cot and lay down to sleep. Sleep was a long time coming as I listened for the sounds of war and once again wondered if I would see the one mortar shell outlined against the star lit night as it came toward me to kill me. A sleep of exhaustion finally gave me relief.

Previous letter continued:

> There is a bird singing on a nearby tree and it's a pretty, short song. Makes me think of home and early mornings, especially when we lived back in Michigan.
> Well, so far I'm still safe and OK. We head off to Camp Anaconda today which is north of Baghdad about fifty miles. After that we'll be headed back to Kuwait. I love you both a lot and miss you a lot.

Oh yeah, while all the action was happening last night there were Bradley tanks rumbling by to go the scene. Very loud and they can go very fast.

I love you both.

6:45 AM We'll be leaving in fifteen minutes. I've eaten part of a MRE for breakfast, lemon pound cake, warm pears, and a soda.

Three people and myself had to load a tuck with water and cases of MREs. Every night they unload the truck so guys can ride in the back to chow but every fucking morning there is no one to load it back up. So I get stuck doing it. I hate stupidity, which is rampant in the Army, and I hate unfairness, which is also rampant in the Army.

It is heating up already and it's not even 7 AM.

8:20 AM In over one hour we have fueled up and traveled about two miles.

8:40 AM We have moved from one side of the airport to the other. We still have not accomplished anything yet. I'm going to try and find something to eat.

11:25 AM We unloaded our stuff and then sat for an hour. Our sergeant ordered us each a hamburger and fries from a burger shop in the airport here. It tasted good after two days of MREs.

We're getting ready to go to Camp Anaconda. I've got my flak vest on and it's fucking hot! I sweat so much yesterday that not only was my t-shirt soaked but the top of my pants were, too. But, I wear the vest for you two girls so I can come home to you.

While we were parked waiting for our burgers a STRYKER (new wheeled armor vehicle that has just arrived over here) hit the tail end of one of our trucks and bent a part off. I watched it and it was cool!

I love you two.

2:30 PM We are at Camp Anaconda. We are supposed to load some Hummers and trailers then back south to unload in Kuwait.

Today I passed a "fresh sheep" roadside market. The Haggis have about three to five sheep around their stand and they butcher one and have the meat up on hooks. It's about a million fucking degrees here, dust everywhere, and they hang their lamb meat on a hook by the side of the road. These people are so fucked!

A pick up truck passed my truck today while I was driving. In the cab were three men and in the back, like the family dog, were the women. I hate every man here. These women need to be liberated.

There must be some fucking heat wave going on because it's never been this hot in Iraq before.

The Army is on this big kick to have us wear our shirts so we're in complete uniform. It's so stupid for them to worry about us wearing our shirts because it's so fucking hot. I hate the military now. None of it makes sense and they don't give a shit about the soldier, just their stupid, no sense rules.

I love you both.

6:55 PM We're loaded and parked for the night. I ate dinner and I am sitting on my cot on a piece of pavement waiting for the fucking temperature to cool down.

It was so hot today that I felt sick again. It's just when the temperature is about 130 degrees and the sun is beating down and I'm working on the truck that I feel that sick. Other than that I just sweat and bitch a lot. The sun just went down and there is finally a breeze, although a warm one. There are huge fast black ants with stingers on their butts running all around the ground. I sure hope they don't bite.

I love you two and miss you a great deal, more than you'll ever know. I hope I come home soon.

Tuesday / 8-5-2003

Where do I start? Oh yeah, in the morning, actually night before. We were at Camp Anaconda getting ready for the night. We were parked in a sandy parking lot, like always. I spotted a building with some cement around it and thought that would be a better place to put our cots for the night than on the back of our trailers as usual. So, three of my friends and myself took our cots over there. We cleaned up and laid down as it was dark. That's when a convoy of Haggis came driving through the sand right next to the building covering us in dust. The trucks came right at us with their headlights on before they turned off into the lot. One of the trucks got stuck and broke it's fuel tank right next to us. So every truck that came after that truck, and there were a lot of them, was detoured through the sand by our cots, dusting us out even more. This went on for over an hour and we kept thinking it would end soon. That's when an Army truck came over the curb and missed one of my friends laying in his cot by just feet. We decided to head back to our trucks and safety.

I put my cot at the end of my trailer and laid and looked at the stars and thought of your two like always. I wondered if I would see the mortar shell outlined against the stars before it blew me to hell. Only a few flares went off during the night, nothing serious.

Got up this morning at 5 AM, like every fucking morning, and drove out. I drove the first half. I drove to Baghdad and around it until we took our first break at noon. That's five hours driving with no stop. Lot's of traffic around Baghdad.

Then we hit the ninety miles of road where there is no road, just dust, heat, and bumps everywhere. I was so tired I actually feel asleep for a few minutes while bouncing around like a rubber ball and, no, I wasn't driving.

There were a lot of hungry people along the way. We threw MREs and a bunch of candy, gum, and some boxes of raisins to the kids. I think I am going to buy a lot of little snacks for the kids on my next mission. It sure made me and my battle-buddy feel better.

Near the end of that stretch of road we lost four HETs. We parked alongside the road while one truck went back to find them. We stood outside our trucks on security while we waited. The Haggis were all over us.

I handed one little girl a dollar because I didn't' have any more food to give out and I couldn't resist her. She never smiled or said anything. She just walked over to her dad and gave it to him. He stuck it in his shirt pocket and didn't even acknowledge me. I hope it helps feed her.

Well, I don't know what's going on with this heat. Usually it's cooler in central Iraq but it's been hot as it's ever been today. If the weather would just break I would feel a lot better. Hopefully it won't matter and I'll be home soon.

I'm back at Tallil Air Base in southern Iraq. It's fucking hot and I can't wait until the sun goes down so it can cool off.

I love you two!

Wednesday / 8-6-2003 / 5:50 AM

What a shitty night. I was so tired and just laid on my cot like a sack of shit for a while because it was so hot. Then I finally feel asleep until midnight when I woke up because the wind had stopped and it was dead, hot air. Oh yeah, and the bugs were biting. I have scabs on both ankles from bites, cuts on both forearms (still don't know how I got those), an ingrown toenail, numerous bites all over. I'm just plain fucking miserable and it's fucking hot already. I am so worn down from this heat. I hope for a break soon. It's getting me down.

I love you both.

1:15 PM We're in Kuwait. We crossed the border about an hour ago. It was a pretty calm trip except for the extreme heat. How hot was it? It was so hot I had to wear my gloves yesterday to hold my M-16. Even the plastic was hot. It was so hot I had to wear my gloves to climb in our truck because the metal would burn my hands. It's so hot I have trouble breathing so I pant like a dog.

I hate this fucking place!

I love you two.

Back in Camp Victory, Kuwait. Safe for now.

Love,
Dad

Letter to School / Wednesday / 8-13-2003

Hey Everyone,

I hope you're ready to greet those fresh, smiling faces. The faces I see in Iraq aren't smiling much anymore.

I hope everyone had a good summer. Mine left a little to be desired

No word on when I get to come home; even the rumors have dried up. I hope it is soon as I am physically and emotionally tired (getting shot at will do that). I miss Ventura and all the good people at school. Hope to see you soon.

Joe B.

Letter Home / Friday / 8-15-2003

Hi Girls,
Well, mission number five for Dad. We're off to Baghdad after a couple of stops. It's 1:15 PM, we always leave at the hottest part of the day, and we're going to pick up lumber for Christ's sake. It's hot as hell and they make us wear our shirts. The Army is so stupid! I hope when I come back from this mission there will be good news about getting out of here. I love you both.
3:50 PM I am at Camp Virginia in Kuwait. We are here to pick up our lumber. Of course, there is no one here and we are sitting in our trucks in about 130 degree temperatures with the wind blowing the sand all over. The wind is so hot it burns my skin. I hate this fucking place!
The camp we are at is almost deserted. I guess they are going to close this camp down soon.
Everything here is so fucked up. People are arguing, fighting, and just basically falling apart. I really feel like I've done my duty and should be coming home. Hauling lumber is not important enough for me to be in this shitty place. This place is so bleak that it's hard for me to believe I'm really here, even after three months.
I love you both!

Saturday / 8-16-2003 / 6:05 AM

What a shitty night's sleep. It was too hot to sleep for me and there was a warm breeze blowing so when I finally fell asleep, I woke up an hour later with dry lips and throat. So, I got up, got a drink and put some lip balm on. By the time I crawled out of my cot, down off the pile of lumber, off the trailer, up on the stack of wood, and back to my cot, I was wide awake. So, I laid in my cot feeling hot and thinking of women for a long while. I didn't sleep much at all last night.
We have about thirty HETs in this convoy. It's pretty big, long, and impressive (and if you weren't my daughters, I'd make a really dirty joke right at this point). The sun has just risen and the temperature is rising already. I'm tired of being hot. I'm tired of sleeping on a cot. I'm tired of shitting in smelly port-a-johns. I'm tired of getting up early. I'm tired of this whole shithole existence. I fucking hate this place!

I love you both.

7:10 AM I just got back from breakfast which consisted of cold eggs and bread toasted on one side only and butter so hard that when you spread it on your toast it just rips the bread.

A thought. If we're hauling lumber, where's the emergency? Why are we here risking our lives for lumber? Seems to me they are just keeping us here for no good reason, except the captain, who is a total asshole, and the 1st Sergeant, who is an even bigger asshole, want a million miles of missions and their promotions on our backs. They are using our blood and sweat to further their careers. I hate them with a passion!

Cracked, Warped Lumber Vs. My Life

Sitting at Camp Virginia in Kuwait. It's 1300 hours and it's hotter than fuck. It seems like we are always sitting in our trucks during the hottest time of the day, always sitting waiting either to leave, load up, or unload. The temperature has to be over 130 degrees again today. We are told that we will be picking up a load of lumber and taking it to BIAP. Of course, there is no one around who knows anything about the load of lumber, so while our fearless leader is off trying to find out the score, we sit and sweat and sweat and sweat. Looking around this place I am amazed that anyone wants anything to do with this land. It's all sand, blowing all day long, only slacking off when evening comes and the sun goes down. There is nothing growing anywhere and no color. I miss color so much. Once, while I was entering Tallil Airbase in Iraq, there were some umbrellas along the road over some tables at a restaurant, and I got all excited because they had color. There were a couple of blue umbrellas and a couple of pink ones. I started to take my camera out of my pocket, which I kept on me at all times in a plastic sandwich bag to keep the sand out of it, and then stopped, wondering why the hell I was going to take a picture of some sand covered umbrellas. It was because of the color. I hadn't seen color in a long time and it was exciting. Weird! Anyway, after looking around at the sand I tried to set up for the night because it became apparent we weren't going to be leaving Camp Virginia anytime soon and night was fast approaching. Of course, once the night did come, someone decided it was time to load up. Some forklifts showed up and we followed them to where the lumber was stacked to get it on our trucks. Using the headlights of the truck behind us and our flashlights we got our HETs ready for the next day's mission to Baghdad. There were a couple things that stuck in my mind that evening. One was the dust that was everywhere as the forklifts loaded the lumber and our trucks moved up in line. It was like a fog in the headlights and beams of the flashlights.

Of course it was all over my clothes, my skin, and in my eyes and teeth as well. Driving back to our place where we were going to stay for the night, we set up our cots again and got ready for the night. I set up my cot on top of the pile of lumber on my trailer thinking I could get a breeze high up there and it would help cool me down as I tried to sleep. Boy, was I wrong. There was no breeze at all that night. Just a heavy heat that drenched me in sweat as I lay on my cot. I kept spraying myself with my water bottle to little effect. After a few missions I discovered that if I drenched my cot in water and laid in it, I would keep cool for up to one half hour. For a few seconds after I covered my body with a mist of water the air would give me a quick cool down. I keep that spray bottle on a book shelf where I can see it every day at home now. It saved my life many times over. I lay in the cot and just sweated. After a while I sat up and just felt totally miserable not being able to sleep and not being able to cool off at all. Another shitty night in this shitty part of the world in this shitty war. After falling asleep finally, I woke up in the middle of the night because I had to take a piss. Now this is when the complete stupidity of me sleeping high on top of the lumber came into full effect. I slipped on my flip-flops, then had to climb down the pile of lumber I was on top of, then climb down off the trailer, then walk a few feet away from the truck and piss in the sand. Then I had to repeat the process of climbing back up to my cot. By the time I was back in my cot I was completely fucking awake. Then I laid there all pissed off, sweating, and fucking miserable, as usual. In the morning I woke up with dry lips and throat because of the dryness of the air. This day was starting out just like all the others, shitty! There are about thirty HETs in this convoy, and that makes for a pretty impressive sight. As we are getting ready to move out, the sun is already out by 5 AM and the temperature is on the rise. Fuck! I hate this place! I'm tired of the heat. I'm tired of the lousy food. I'm tired of sleeping on a cot. I'm tired of having to walk into a smelly port-a-john to take a shit. I'm tired of getting up early. I'm tired of being tired. I'm tired of wondering if I will see another day or if this one will be last. I'm tired of this whole shithole existence. I go to breakfast hoping things will improve. Cold eggs and toast only toasted on one side with butter so hard it rips the bread as I try to spread it. But, at least it's not a MRE. That's what I have to look forward to for the next several days on the road to Baghdad. The idea of taking warped, cracked lumber to BIAP is starting to wear on me. Why am I risking my life to take some fucking lumber that on one would use in the states to Baghdad? Is my life worth this load? Is it that fucking important? If I get killed on this mission will they tell my family that I died for some fucking warped, cracked lumber? What a waste it would be. Next stop is Navstar on the border of Iraq and Kuwait. We drive off into the sand

through the sand berms that mark our route out the gate and toward Iraq and Baghdad. Goddamn Army!

Previous letter continued:

Even my friends are starting to get on my nerves. I've been stuck with these people for over six months now and ninety-nine percent of these people I would never hang out with in civilian life.

I still can't figure out the stupid rule that we are supposed to wear our blouse (that's what they call the outer shirt we wear) all the time. Last week a soldier in the 3rd COSCOM (unit I am in) died from heat stroke in a convoy. Did anyone consider that wearing that damn shirt had something to do with it? Put a flak vest over it and you've got a personal sauna. These people are ridiculous. Also, both my sets of desert uniforms are the winter style. My material doesn't "breathe" like the summer ones. So, not only am I here for the hottest time of the year, but I have to wear winter uniforms. Pretty sad from the "greatest Army on the Earth." If people only knew how shitty the National Guard treats their troops. We get killed over here, too. I certainly will tell people how shitty we were treated when I get back.

We're not leaving until 8 AM. We will go to Navstar, the last stop before we cross the border into Iraq. Then on to Tallil Air Base about halfway between Baghdad and the border. I sure hope the heat wave is over up there and it's a little cooler. One guy told me that a couple weeks ago they had a temperature reading of 148 degrees at our base in Kuwait. I don't know if that's true but it sure feels like it sometimes.

I love both of you a lot.

9:20 AM We're still sitting here at Camp Virginia in Kuwait. We've eaten breakfast, lined up the trucks (thirty of them), and are waiting on getting our cases of water. We'll be getting a late start which means driving in the heat of the day. Ugh! On the side of our truck I wrote in chalk, "One Week End A Month, MY ASS!" This refers to the National Guard's advertisement of only working one week end a month. I also wrote "Ventura, CA." and "California Dreaming" and over the huge tires, "Hagi Crusher" with an arrow pointing to the tire. War humor, I guess. Guess I'll sit and sweat some more.

I will try my hardest to call you, Christie, for your birthday. I am so sorry I won't be there. I doubt I'll make yours, Jennie. I do love you both and never want to be away from you again where I can't at least come see you on your birthdays. I love you two.

5:10 PM Still hot as hell. The wind burns my skin. We are stopped in southern Iraq. We just test fired our weapons.

8 PM I'm back. I was writing about how we tested our weapons. I was standing by the truck as we were stopped. Whenever we stop we have to get out and "guard" the convoy. All of a sudden there is a blast about one hundred yards away from me. I ducked and started looking around for whatever the hell did that. It turns out everyone was firing their weapons to make sure they worked before we went into bad guy territory. The big bang was one guy testing his grenade launcher. Of course, they didn't tell our truck so I thought we were under attack like the last time. Anyway, good thing we did because I had trouble getting my weapon to fire. I finally got it working and shot one round, then a burst of three into a berm.

Coffins. Did I tell you that people drive around with coffins on top of their cars? They do and I'm sure there are bodies in them because of the blankets they put on the coffins.

Coffins

As I drive down the roads of Iraq, every once in a while a car will pass us or come the other way toward us with a coffin on it's roof. They are usually covered with a blanket that is flapping in the wind. The coffins are tied on the roof and I always wonder who is in the coffin? Where are they going? Why in the hell are they tied on the roof of a car? What a weird country with weird customs. I want to be home.

A car with a coffin on top, blanket blowing.

Previous letter continued:

10 PM I have already been asleep once and now I'm not. Let's discuss the insanity I have to live with the past six months. While I lay on my cot, to my right a guy is having a conversation with someone far enough away that he's almost screaming. To the left of me someone is playing their radio at full blast. To the front of me there are five or six assholes who are getting drunk from the Hagi whiskey they bought outside the gate.

Now two drunks are puking near the end of my trailer. Another drunk is yelling that he wants to fight, and lucky me, it's all right next to where I am sleeping. I hate people! I am so sick of self-centered, selfish assholes. I fight every day to hang on to my sanity. I hate this fucking place and all the assholes in it!

I love you two.

Insanity

Tallil Air Base in southern Iraq. We have parked for the night. HETs parked close together because our trucks are so large and parking space is so small. I have a truck on either side of me and one to my rear near the trailer. My cot is set up on the trailer and I'm ready to sleep for the night because tomorrow is another long, hot day on the way to BIAP. After sleeping for a while, I am awaken by a disturbance. As I sit up on my cot to see what the hell woke me up, I am engulfed by the insanity around me. Someone to my right is having a conversation with someone who is so far away that he is screaming. To my left someone is playing their boom box loud enough for everyone to hear within a quarter mile. Of course it's some punk rock shit that is loud, ridiculous, and ear-grating. Right at the end of my trailer there are five or six assholes talking loudly, drinking the Hagi whiskey they had bought earlier at the gate. They are totally drunk and out of control. One of the drunks walks about ten feet from me and stats puking. The others come over to watch and laugh, which causes another one to start puking. There are now two puddles of puke within ten feet of my cot. Music is blaring, a man is screaming his speech to someone he cannot see, and the drunks are puking and laughing. One of them decides he wants to kick someone's ass. I'm not sure if he cared who it was; he just wanted to kick some ass. I am blessed this night as the show is all around me and within ten to thirty feet of my cot. What a great way to fight a war! As I wait for the show to die down, I remember what it is about people that makes me hate them sometimes. Now, to top it off, the mosquitoes are out and I have to get my bug juice on. I lather it on, sit on my cot, write a letter home to my girls telling of what is happening around me at that moment, and just feel miserable. After the drunks pass out and get quiet and the loud talker talks himself out, only the music is left to keep me up. I walk over to the music and the drunk that is playing it and ask him to turn it down so I can go back to sleep. To my surprise I don't have to fight him; rather, he turns the music down. I climb back onto the trailer and into my cot and lay there thinking how crazy this place it. As usual, before sleep comes, I stare at the stars and think of my two daughters and miss them with all my heart. I also wonder if I will see the mortar round before it blows me to hell and sleep finally comes. Another shitty night in a shitty country in a shitty war. Fuck! I'm tired.

Previous letter continued:

Sunday / 8-17-2003 / 6 AM

Happy birthday, Christie! I am so sad that I can't be there with you. There are some things about this activation that are just wrong and me missing your birthday is one of them. Looks like I'll miss yours, too, Jennie. I feel terrible about missing your birthdays, but it's out of my hands.

Birthdays

On the road to Baghdad and it's my youngest daughter's birthday. I think of the past birthdays when there was always cake and ice cream and presents and laughter. This time there is none of that. There is only heat, a long drive down dangerous roads, and an intense feeling of sadness that I cannot be with my daughter on this special day because of this stupid war. I can't even get to a phone to call her and wish her a happy birthday and tell her that I am thinking of her and missing her with all my heart. I can't tell her I love her. Back at home that is taken for granted, hugging your children, telling them you love them, seeing their faces every day. Here, it's a dream and a wish. Nothing makes me feel sadder than thinking of my family while I am here. Their letters are like gifts from the gods when they arrive. I usually read them a couple times over because I wanted to relive every detail they write about and pretend I am there. It's my daughter's birthday and I'm driving a HET to Baghdad while people are shooting at me, and at any moment an IED (improvised explosive device or a mine) could end my life, or destroy it forever. This is not the way to celebrate a birthday of your child.

Previous letter continued:

It finally got quiet last night after the drunk assholes got done puking and yelling and finally went to sleep (or passed out). I finally went over to the guy and his radio and asked him to turn it down. He was drunk, too, but he turned it down. I got about six hours of good sleep and woke up with my sleeping bag on because it actually got cool last night. Oh yeah, I had to put "mosquito juice" on last night because I started to get eaten. The never-ending nightmare continues. I hate people and I hate this shithole of a place. I've never been as tired and frustrated in all of my life.

I miss you both and love you both tremendously.

We go to BIAP today. That stands for "Baghdad International Airport. This is the nervous part of the trip. I promise to keep my eyes open and be careful.

I went to breakfast riding in the back of a LFMTV (large family of medium truck vehicle; stupid, huh)? It's a bumpy, jerky ride, but it got me to sub-par food, which is par here.

I have my shirt hanging on the side window of the truck to block out the sun because the sun is beating on me and it's hot already.

Opps, gotta take a shit; to the smelly port-a-john.

Love you both.

8:40 AM Happy birthday Christie! I hope you have fun with the guitar I gave you the money for.

The one thing that bothers me about this mission is that I'm going in harm's way for lumber. I don't understand how lumber is worth any of our lives. I think it's time they send the National Guard home and let the active Army do this bullshit.

Off to my left are hangers that have the tank buster jets called Warthogs. They can blow up anything on the battlefield and usually do. To my right is flat, brown land littered with garbage. We're getting fuel and it takes thirty HETs a while to fuel up. Hot already.

Love you two!

5:10 PM Well, we made it to BIAP. Nothing happened. I only flipped off two people (they made the bad gestures first). I waved to the kids, especially the girls. I feel so sorry for them because I never see any girls over the age of ten or so unless they are covered in black. I hate everything about this part of the world except the women; they don't stand a chance.

Finished eating dinner and I'm waiting to find out if we unload our lumber tonight or not. Then we sleep. Last time we were here we got mortared, so it may be an interesting night.

I love you both.

7:10 PM My cot is up on the lumber on the trailer. I'm sitting in my shorts and the sun is going down at the Baghdad Airport. One of the biggest planes I've ever seen just flew overhead. Actually, it's circling for the third time. Bats are flying overhead.

They eat mosquitoes, which is good. Guys are drinking beer, whiskey, showering, shitting, all getting ready for another night in hell. I wonder what tonight will bring. Last time we got mortared, a building on fire, fuel truck hit, tanks, tracers, etc. Hopefully tonight will be quiet.

    Love you both.

Bats

Setting up for the night at BIAP. The cots are out, the coolers are close at hand, my squirt bottle is handy, and I'm in my shorts and flip-flops. It's dusk and the bats have come out. They fly a few feet over our heads and someone always takes a stone and throws it up in the air to see them quickly veer to avoid the stone. It's a form of entertainment for a few minutes until we lose interest and go about doing some other mundane thing to pass the time. I always am thankful for the bats because I know they are eating some of the mosquitoes that will keep me awake tonight when I so badly need to sleep.

Previous letter continued:

Monday / 8-18-2003 / 6:30 AM

    I hope you had a good birthday Christie. I haven't been able to get to a phone and I may not until we get back. Sorry baby.

    It was cool last night. We didn't get mortared, just a bunch of flares going off. I slept good for the first time on this trip. That's one benefit of going into central Iraq; the temperature drops, except for that last mission. The days are still miserable, but the nights are better. I even took another shower this AM and got goose bumps that I've missed so much.

Showers at BIAP

Right after the war our showers on the road during missions were out of water cans or water bottles. The water jugs would be stored on the back of the tractor part of our HETs. When we were down for the night, we would wait for dark, because we always had women on the missions and were being polite, and then take our showers. We'd park our trucks close to one another because they were so big we needed to conserve space and so that we were close enough to help each other out. One person would climb up on the back of the tractor and lay the water can on its side with the spout facing out over the edge. One person would strip down with flip-flops and soap. That person would stand under the can while the person on top would unscrew the cap and let the water flow out slowly. First you'd get wet, stop the water flow, soap up, and then rinse off. Everyone tried to use as little water as possible so that everyone could get a turn and the water would last. If someone spent too much time under the water, the others would let him know right away with a strong statement filled with obscenities. If a water can was not available or if there wasn't anyone around to help, you turned to the water bottles that were carried by the cases on the trucks. You'd take a knife and poke a few slits in the cap of the water bottle. The first bottle would be to get wet. Then you soap up and use two more bottles to rinse off. If you used one bottle, there always seemed to be a little soap somewhere that you didn't get. You get enough rashes in the desert without leaving soap on your body to get another one. After a while my children had sent me a plastic camping shower that I had bought before I shipped out. We would tie it to the hand winch that we had on our HETs for winching tires on our trailers. We would raise the bag with the shower hose dangling underneath it. This was the best shower situation we had on the road on our missions until BIAP got outdoor showers near the new DFAC (dining facility) south of the main runway. Not only could we park near a place to eat, but we could now walk to a shower that was outside and unlimited water. Most showers in Iraq were unsatisfying and really didn't get you clean. But these new ones at BIAP were like being in heaven. You walked over a sea of stones that had been laid down to keep the dust down. Then you opened the wooden door, undressed and hung your clothes over the door, and turned on the water. It was great! You could keep the water going even while soaping up. The shower heads were pretty beat up and didn't let much water out, and a few were missing completely, but if you got one that worked, you felt the gods smiling down on you. For once in Iraq you could feel clean for a few minutes, at least until you reached the dusty sand again. Once, on a mission to BIAP, I went over there in the morning before we left on that day's trip to take a shower in the morning. I had not had a shower in the morning for months. It felt good, and the best part was I actually got cold in the morning air. Imagine, goose-bumps in the summer in Iraq. It was the best, and I always wanted to thank the soldiers that built those showers in Iraq at the Baghdad Airport in the summer of 2003. Another memorable shower was early in the summer, again at BIAP. This time we parked our HETs right on the tarmac of the airport. We were there to pick up some vehicles of the Third Infantry Division. They were on their way home after being through the war and months before that. While on that tarmac our LT (lieutenant) found an opened container somewhere on base that had apples, watermelon, and plumps that were COLD! After sitting on the tarmac in temperatures over 120 degrees all day, the cold fruit was a miracle. We ate until we couldn't hold anymore in our stomachs and still tried to shove more in. It was too good to stop because we never got cold fruit in Iraq. After the feast and the sun setting, we set up our shower for the night. We hung our camper shower off the small crane, stripped down and cleaned off. I was on the tarmac at the Baghdad Airport in Iraq in a war zone completely naked. I had a friend take a picture because I didn't want to forget that moment. After my picture several others did the same. Proof of naked American soldiers in Baghdad at war. Great picture! Great night, except for the fact we were halfway around the world from our homes.

Previous letter continued:

We're suppose to unload our lumber this morning and then head to Camp Anaconda, which is north of Baghdad, to get some more stuff to take south. That will mean another day to our mission. Rats! I want to get back and see if anything happened about getting out of here. I would love to come home.

Last night there were planes and helicopters flying all over the place, but I was so tired that once I feel asleep, that was it.

I am drinking a soda with ice I took from the mess hall in a cup. We didn't get any ice yesterday so all our drinks are warm. I hope today is better.

Well, girls, things just keep repeating. The missions are basically the same as well as the days and the heat. I hope it ends soon.

I love you both!

1:50 PM Unloaded, finally, and we are headed to Camp Anaconda. Didn't do anything except sit in the heat of the truck. My body is covered in sweat. My arms look like I've put cooking oil on them. Always hot . . . always hot . . . now I have to wear my flak vest, helmet, and feel the hot air blowing in the truck. Man, I hate this!

Love you both.

Tuesday / 8-19-2003 / 6 AM

We got to Anaconda after about two hours. I think I'm going a little nuts over here. I wanted to shoot a Hagi today. No special reason, just felt like killing one. We almost hit a guy crossing the street. He walked slowly across and we were going about 40 MPH in the convoy; we don't slow down and we certainly don't stop, and we missed him by inches. Also, we will ram cars, buses, vans, and trucks off the road if they get in our way. I flipped off two guys yesterday. I have a lot of hate for the male population here in Islam nations. I could kill one of these guys and not loose a second of sleep over it. I feel tremendous sorrow over the situation of the women here. I see the little girls in colorful dresses hopping up and down, waving, smiling, and then at a certain age, they disappear and the only time you see them they are covered in black from head to toe. Any male who lives in the Middle East can go straight to hell! I have a new strong hate for another system of the world and every man/boy who is a part of it.

Only a few flares last night. Things seem to be settling down, at least from my perspective.

We stayed in a dusty place last night. I took a shower by poking holes in the plastic top of three water bottles and spraying it over me. It's not the best way to get clean but it works.

I had a beer last night, made in Holland, sold by Haggis along the road. It wasn't bad but I swear I was a little looped after only one beer. Out of practice.

The sun is rising showing a nice haze of dust, burning shit, and whatever else is in this fucked up country.

Sun Rise In Camp Anaconda

As I awake from my cot on the back of my trailer the sun is rising. It's just peeking through the smoke from the burning shit can that's about twenty feet away, causing a reddish flow in the haze. Ah! The beauty of Iraq!

Previous letter continued:

We load up this AM and then back to BIAP. At least where we stay there we have showers, shitters, and the chow hall close by. I hate this fucking place!

I love you both and miss you like crazy!

Oh, I forgot to tell you. Last night we heard a shot close by. It turned out it was someone who accidentally shot a round off (one of our guys). You should have seen everyone freeze and look around. I guess I have changed somewhat to fit my situation.

I love you two!

The Shot

We're getting ready for another night on the road. Setting up cots, getting the coolers filled with Hagi ice and sodas. I'm getting into my shorts and flip-flops and filling up my spray bottle, getting my toilet paper handy and my shaving kit for the morning. Everything is in place, and we are settling

down for our evening bull-shit session when all of sudden there is a shot! Everyone freezes because the shot is very close and we are in the middle of the base where no one should be shooting at anything. Some just stand. Some grab their weapons. Some duck down under the trucks at whatever part they are near. We all wait quietly to hear or see what will happen next. Someone comes out from the line of trucks parked next to ours and tells us that he accidentally discharged his weapon. We relax and go back to our business of getting ready to sleep in the heat. But for one brief moment we are reminded again of where we are and what we are in danger of, and that is of being killed.

Previous letter continued:

7:45 AM We're waiting to drive and load our trucks. They were burning shit in a can so I took a picture. It would be hard to describe what it looks like so I figured "a picture is worth a thousand words." It's exactly like in the movies of war in Viet Nam. I gotta fuel the trucks up.

Love you both.

11:45 AM Loaded! Man did I sweat. My t-shirt was soaked with sweat. We drove to chow and I ate tacos. Not bad.

Now I'm sitting in the truck waiting to leave for BIAP and I'm dripping sweat.

Did I tell you that any book, or for that matter, writing tablet, magazine, etc. that has the pages glued together come apart from the heat over here? When you read a novel you have to put a rubber band around it to keep it together. Magazine pages just fall apart and this tablet I'm writing on is all loose pages.

Rubber Bands and Books

Any book that I see has a rubber band around it. The heat is so unbearable that even books hate it. The glue melts in the heat and the pages come undone. If you don't have a rubber band to wrap your book in you're probably not going to be able to finish it. Writing pads would come apart in the heat as well as magazines. Nothing was safe from the heat in Iraq. I once got a package that contained a bag of gummy bears. It was one of the most beautiful sights I've ever seen, because when I opened the package, it had all melted together and the colors were so vivid and bright, it looked like a modern art painting. When we worked on our trucks we had to wear our gloves, even though the temperature was over 120 degrees. If you touched the metal of the truck, you would get burned. I forgot one day while I reached for the gas cap on our truck to begin to refuel it up. I remembered about wearing the gloves real quick when my hand touched that gas cap. One day it was so hot that I had to wear my gloves to hold my weapon. Even the plastic was burning my hands. When you stood on the payment of a road or the sand that was everywhere, the heat radiated through the soles of your shoes and burned the bottom of your feet. If you didn't drink your bottle of water within a few minutes of pulling it out of the cooler, it would be too hot to drink. If you put anything plastic on the ledge by the front window of the truck, it would melt to the metal and stay there forever. I sometimes wonder if that baggie of sunflower seeds is still melted to the front of my HET. To keep cool on the convoys, or anywhere for that matter, I would pour some water into my helmet and let it sit for about one minute. After a minute of so I would dump the water on my head and it would actually be cool. My battle-buddy loved to watch me dump the water on my head and soak myself every few minutes. He thought I was nuts, but I was just trying to keep cool. You could always tell the 'Newbies' when you were in Kuwait. They would have this stupid cloth around their neck that was purchased at the PX. If you soak it in water for a few minutes and put it around your neck, it was supposed to cool you off. Only the people who were new in country spent their money on this useless item. I only kept mine for about a week as I was a 'Newbie' once, too. One thing I did do constantly was to soak a 'do-rag' and hold it out for a few seconds and then put it on my head under my helmet. This seemed to create a little air conditioning effect around my face and neck for a few minutes. My spray bottle probably saved my life over there. I took this wherever I went. I would spray my face and arms and head over and over again. The slight coolness for the few seconds was heaven to me in hell. My battle-buddy and I were driving down a road, and as usual it was hot as hell. All of a sudden we heard a shot. I looked out the window and he did the same, as we both said, "Who's doing the shooting?" After a few minutes we relaxed again and then heard another shot. We both starting yelling, again, "Who's doing the shooting?" This went on for few miles and about twenty minutes. We couldn't figure out who was taking shots at us every few minutes and if they were following us or we were just being unlucky passing all these people trying to kill us. Another shot went off, only this time the spray of soda hit my battle-buddy on his arm. Turns out the case of soda we had on the back seat had gotten so swollen with the heat, the cans were exploding. After a few minutes of laughing at ourselves and throwing the swollen cans of sodas out the window, we returned to the mundane job of driving down a road with nothing but sand as far as the eye could see and heat that would blister our skin. Keeping cool rated right up there with trying to stay alive in Iraq. It was just too damn hot for humans over there.

—

Previous letter continued:

Too hot to write anymore. I'm going to just sit here and sweat.
Love you both.

Wednesday / 8-20-2003 / 6:20 AM

I don't think I have ever sweated as much as I did yesterday. Between loading the truck, sitting for two hours in the heat of the day in our big metal trucks, and driving to Baghdad with a flak vest on, I sweated all fucking day. Luckily I had some powered drink with me because I needed it.

The trip here to BIAP was uneventful except for when one of our trucks hit a Hagi fuel truck along the road and ripped open its gas tank so fuel was pouring out on the street. The drivers here have no rules. They park any fucking where on the road and then cars/trucks are sticking out in traffic. So, one of them paid yesterday.

Oh yeah, I almost hit a car full of asshole Haggis when they pulled in front of me and slowed down. Another foot and I would have sent those assholes to Allah. I can still picture one dumbfuck staring out the rear window looking up at me as I came close to his bumper.

I slept up high on our load and there was no fucking breeze at all. I took a picture, so you'll see. And just two nights ago I got cold here. Last night, nothing. Fuck! I hate this place.

We head back to Camp Victory today. We should get halfway and stay at Tallil Airbase.

I love you both and miss you like crazy.

4 PM I'm at Tallil Airbase. Let me give you an idea of how hot it gets here. I had a case of soda in the truck, outside the cooler. It got so hot that they started popping, of course, sounding like gunshots. Since their sound of popping was a bad sound I kept looking around trying to figure out where the shots were coming from. It wasn't until my battle-buddy got sprayed that we found out the cause of the sounds. Nice fucking place, huh?

I'm sitting in my shorts on a case of water in the shade of my truck. There is still more than two hours until the sun goes down and until that happens I will sweat and swear. Did I mention I hate this place?

I had to drive on a narrow two-lane road. You remember that our trailers don't fit in one lane because they are too wide? Well, it took over two hours to drive that stretch of road and every second was nerve wracking. Especially when other large Army trucks passed going the other way. I swear our outside mirrors were scrapping. Very dangerous and I'm glad that part is over with.

I want you to know that every day of a mission when I'm getting ready to drive, I check my helmet. I make sure my lucky characters that you both gave me are secured on the helmet. I kiss my fingers and pat them on the characters for good luck. Once in a while, during the day, I will reach behind me and squeeze both characters and pretend I'm hugging you two.

And today I not only wore my flak vest and helmet, I even put my seat belt on while I was driving down that narrow road. I'm probably the only guy in Iraq that wore his seatbelt, but, I'm being safe.

I love you guys!

6:45 PM The sun is down. I'm back on top of our load on the trailer. I'm pretty far up for a guy who's afraid of heights. At least there is a breeze tonight. I still have to shower. I'll use the water bottles again. I'm really tired. I hope I can sleep tonight.

I love you two stinkers!

Thursday / 8-21-2003 / 5:20 AM

It's a little cool right now and it feels good. It's probably only about 85 or 90 degrees, but the sun is coming up and it will heat up quick. Gotta put my cot away and bags and get ready to head back to Kuwait today.

I think of you two constantly and want to be home with you. I love you both.

6:35 AM This morning's breakfast consisted of grape jelly so warm that it was in a totally liquid state, on something they call wheat bread potato sticks (the highlight of the meal), and fudge brownie cake that I took only one bite of before throwing it away. Yes, it was a MRE breakfast. It's fucking hot already. I can't wait to be in the air conditioned tent tonight. It will feel so good to be so cold.

I miss you and love you two more than you will ever know. I want to be there to share our lives.

1:50 PM It is so fucking hot I can hardly breathe. I've had a headache for about two hours now. We are sitting in our trucks roasting along this roadway just across the border in Kuwait. One of our soldiers has a heat injury so we have been sweating our asses off not moving for about an hour. I hate the Army and I hate the stupid people in it. And I hate this fucking part of the world more than anything.

I threw food to all the little girls along the road on the way here.

Nothing happened on this trip. I don't know the latest in the news but it sure seems calmer from my point of view.

I can't wait to get back tonight so I can finally cool off in my air conditioned tent. I've only spent one night in the new tent so far.

I love you both!

I'm back and I'm safe!

I love you guys!

Dad

Card to school / Wednesday / 8-27-2003

Hey Everyone,
I just sitting in the MWR tent (moral, welfare, and recreation). I've been watching movies for about four hours in a row. They put one movie in after another. I worked this AM on the truck. Now, it's fun time.
I have had six days off from missions and it's been a little more relaxing.
Still no word on a return date. Everyone is tired and ready to come home. There are all kinds of rumors that we may have to spend a whole year here. That's scary because one of our trucks was hit with a RPG (rocket propelled grenade) north of Baghdad today. They hit the trailer and the two guys got out with minor burns, but it makes me wonder about this place. I just drove down that same road last week.

This is one of our trucks that was hit with a PRG (rocket propelled grenade)
in northern Iraq. We had brought it back to Kuwait on another truck.

I hope you are enjoying the early school year. I wish I was there. I miss all your smiling faces.

Joe B.

Port-a-johns Cleaning

While I was at Camp Victory in Kuwait, time passed very slowly. There was letter writing, talking, listening to music, and just laying on the cot being

miserable in the heat. One "low-light" of the day was when the Haggis came to clean the port-a-johns. Outside every few tents there would be a group of six to eight port-a-johns for the troops to use. There were about fifty people to each tent, so usually about two hundred soldiers used one set of port-a-johns. It's hard to describe what human waste smells like after being baked in temperatures over 130 degrees, but it is one of the worst smells I've ever experienced. The first month and a half that I spent in Iraq and Kuwait, I was gagging all the time. Trying to use the port-a-johns during this time became a great challenge to me. I devised a procedure that allowed me to take care of business when I needed. I would get my roll or toilet paper in my hand, and just before I stepped into the port-a-john, I would take a little part of the toilet paper, wad it up, and shove it up my nose. I would do this to both nostrils. Then I would take a small cigar and light it. I did not smoke the cigar, I simply held it under my nose while I was in the shitter. Taking care of business in Iraq and Kuwait never took too long as drinking water all day, every day, helped keep things "loose." After taking care of business, I would quickly take the toilet paper out of my nose, throw it where I had just been sitting, and leave. I would then rub the cigar out on a cement block that kept the ropes of the tent taunt in the sand until it was needed for next time. When the Haggis came to clean the port-a-johns, they would drive up with an odd looking truck, with a pump and a large tank on the back. A couple Haggis would always be sitting on the outside or hanging on the side of the truck. They would then pump out the waste, spray the shitters with a high pressure washer, and leave. The part that made this memorable every day was the STINK! The smell was the worst smell ever imagined by anyone. Everyone in the tent, even though they couldn't see the truck, knew what was happening when the Haggis came to clean the port-a-johns. For a few minutes everything stopped, people covered their noses, or just got out of the tent and went upwind of the cleaning. I have been sitting in the tent and stuck toilet paper up my nose to wait the stink out. When the Haggis came through the camp to clean the shitters, everyone was grateful that it was these people that did this distasteful job, and not us. It sure was an experience that I don't want to have again.

Letter home / Saturday / 8-30-2003

Hi Girls,

Thought I'd drop you a note. I'm sitting under cammo netting outside of sick call. They are making me start the process all over again to try and get more medical information before they do anything about my knee and feet.

The weather actually seems to be changing, although it still gets hot, it seems a little less so. Usually by now, 8 AM, it's unbearable already, but it's just "hot" right now. I hope I'm not here long enough for the "seasons."

Things seem to be getting better here as far as living conditions. It's still far too dangerous, though. We have air conditioning in the tent and I actually sleep in my sleeping bag now. Some nights I actually turn the air conditioner off that's right over my cot because it's too cold. Can you imagine that?

Yesterday the guys and I were in the chow hall and we were cold. The temperature was 85 degrees and we were cold. Do you think our blood has thinned? I'll be freezing when I finally get back to Ventura, but I'll be happy.

We have a tent with phones, computers, and movies now, too. So, the base camp is much better. To bad when we go north to Iraq it's so unstable.

As soon as I get done here I have to go back to the tent and neaten my area. It's so hard to live out of bags, boxes, and containers all the time. I have too much shit to fit under my cot, so I have shit all around it. I don't know where I'm gonna put everything, but I will figure it out.

We have mice and rats in our tent. I caught one in a trap by my bunk the other day and took a picture. Then, of course, I threw the rat away. We catch two to three a day now.

The great hunter gets another kill.

Monday / 9-1-2003 / Labor Day

I can't call because the phones are down. As soon as I can I will call. I'm just biding my time until I can come home to you two. The nightmare never ends.

Tomorrow I go to the doctor for the discussion. We'll see what happens.

I love you two.

I'm standing in the rain in Germany, after leaving Iraq just two days ago. Happiness!

Sunday / 9-7-2003

I flew out of Kuwait to Germany on a Med-Evac flight. After spending one day in Landstuhl Hospital I was sent back to the states for further medical testing. The knee that I had injured prior to being sent to Iraq had become a problem, as well as both my feet becoming infected and injured.

Tuesday / 9-9-2003 through 3-4-2004

After spending seven months in Ft. Lewis, Washington rehabbing my knee and other issues, I was sent home for good.

Several months after being sent home, I was retired out of the Army National Guard with over twenty-one years of service. I had spent close to four years on active duty with the remainder in the National Guard.

Military History

Although I was drafted in 1969 during the Viet Nam War, I spent my two years in Germany.

In 1990 I was activated for the Gulf War, but was sent home when my father had and stroke and ended up dying. I did not go to the Gulf War.

Right after 9/11 I was activated for Operation Aero Safe. I served at the Santa Barbara Airport in California for six months as added security.

I finally got my war in 2003 with Operation Iraqi Freedom. This is my record of that time in training as well as in country.

Final Thoughts

I was sent back to Ft. Lewis, Washington after flying back from Iraq. I spent the next six months talking to a shrink for what the Army calls, "Crying jags." After raising two daughters it seems I had a little trouble with the sights of the little girls over in Iraq and their hopeless lives in my eyes. I also spent time rehabbing my right knee that was injured in training for Iraq. I was finally medically discharged from active duty in March of 2004.

Life after Iraq was a little shaky at first. I had trouble driving down the highway and going under the overpasses. I was always looking on the overpass for people or by the sides of it. It was a habit from Iraq that took a while to lose. It was also hard just to drive the car after driving the HET for so long. Every time I saw a pothole I would get nervous. It took some time to lose the fear of the road.

The first July 4th I spent at home after being in Iraq was a terrible night. When the fireworks started going off in the neighborhood I actually went and sat on a small landing on my stairway. I sat in the corner in the dark for a long time. I kept telling myself that it was just fireworks and it wasn't mortar rounds going off. I just couldn't move. Every 4th of July since I have not enjoyed the fireworks and spent my night in the house. It's just not the same anymore for me no matter what I tell myself.

I have always been proud of serving in Iraq. After being drafted in 1969 during the Viet Nam War and spending my two years in Germany I had always felt that I missed out on my war. I know that sounds funny to people, but it was something I dealt with over the years. After finally being sent to the war in Iraq I felt that I had, at last, done my duty to my country.

I went to the companies welcome home ceremony. As I saw the old faces just back from Iraq I felt very out of place. I sat in the back at the end of the line and knew I didn't belong with them anymore. Just before the ceremony was about to begin I snuck out of the same gym that we had sat in listening to the general before we were activated, got into my car and drove back home. It was their day, not mine.

My daughters tell me that I had aged about ten years when I came back from Iraq. My body was never the same as I have had trouble with my right knee and both feet every day since being over in Iraq. I am now a disabled veteran.

Memories of Iraq and my time spent there are with me every day. I have several items out for display in my home. I sometimes stand and look at them, sometimes get the photo album out and relive some of the moments and experiences I lived in Iraq. Was it worth it? I can't answer that. Only time and history will tell.

LaVergne, TN USA
09 December 2010
208113LV00006B/36/P